The Mountains and the Sky

The Mountains

and the Sky

Lorne E. Render

Glenbow-Alberta Institute
McClelland and Stewart West

Copyright © 1974 by Glenbow-Alberta Institute

ALL RIGHTS RESERVED
ISBN 0—7712—1001—2

For permission to reprint the following material, grateful acknowledgement is made to the copyright holders and publishers.

William Blackwood and Sons Ltd. for *Collected Poems* by Moira O'Neill.

The Viking Press for *Wolf Willow* by Wallace Stegner.

American Heritage Publishing Co. for "When the Wild Northern Boundary Stretched to the Sea a Government Artist Recorded the Rugged Surveying Job", in *American Heritage*.

Adam and Charles Black for *Canada* by William Wilfred Campbell.

John Aylen for *Walter J. Phillips* by Duncan Campbell Scott.

Winnipeg Art Gallery for *H. Eric Bergman* by Ferdinand Eckhart.

Saskatchewan Archives Office for "James Henderson of the Qu'Appelle Valley" by Arthur Hayworth in *Saskatchewan History*.

Clarke Irwin Ltd. for *Growing Pains* by Emily Carr.

Vancouver Art Gallery for *Max Bates in Retrospect* 1921-71.

The publishers have made every effort to obtain permission from copyright holders whose work has been reproduced in this book. We sincerely apologize for any inadvertent omissions.

McClelland and Stewart West
Printed and Bound in Canada

Contents

	Introduction	9
1	The Expedition Artists	17
2	The West Visited	47
3	The First Residents	89
4	Contemporary Views	181
	Reference Notes	216
	Bibliography	217
	List of Works	219
	Index	222

Preface

Glenbow-Alberta Institute was established in 1966, when Eric L. Harvie and his family gave the Glenbow Foundation to the people of Alberta as a centennial gift. In the years since its inception, Glenbow has acquired the most valuable collection of western Canadian art and cultural and historical artifacts in existence. The Art Department alone has approximately 22,000 works, which include sculpture, porcelain, crystal, drawings, water colours, and paintings. The greater part of the collection deals with the pictorial history and art of the prairies and mountains, and forms an outstanding record of a picturesque land and its people. The paintings selected for this book are only a small proportion of the total number.

Every painting in The Mountains and the Sky is from Glenbow's collection. All measurements are given in inches, with the horizontal dimension listed first.

A number of people contributed time and energy in order to make this book possible. I would like to express my sincere thanks to H. A. Dempsey, Director of History for Glenbow, for his advice on many historical aspects; to Bruce W. Ferguson, Assistant Curator, and Andrew Oko, Curatorial Assistant, whose help was invaluable, and the Art Department, for their cooperation; to the Photography Department, and in particular Ron Marsh, who spent a great deal of time in providing excellent photographs of all the paintings; to Elspeth MacRae, my secretary, who typed the manuscript; to J. A. Hammond, Executive Vice-President of Glenbow, whose energy and foresight brought about the close cooperation between Glenbow and McClelland and Stewart; and finally to my family, for their patience and understanding during the writing of this book.

Introduction

The power of the land irresistably dominates those who come to western Canada. The forcefulness of the environment can be profound, subtle or romantic. One reacts to the infinite prairies, the rolling hills, the hard mountains, and the immense sky in a very personal fashion. This quality of the West is unique, of the land changing and re-changing, from proportions that are measurable and definite, no larger than a man himself, to a scale which is almost beyond imagining.

Rich in forms, space, light, and colours, the West is a continually changing panorama. Overhead, the sky is an endless canopy. Abruptly it is cut by the flat prairie horizon line or the jagged Rocky Mountains. The *surroundingness* of space is total, overwhelming. Everywhere the colours seem unnatural - the rich green, gold, and white, and the incredible sky, like an intense blue shell covering the universe. There is solitude and loneliness, for those who seek it, from which emerges a bond between man and nature. Even in the Rockies the sense of space is unlimited, but in an upward direction. The scale is never confining or intimate.

The forms in the western landscape provide endless variations. From one vantage point the prairies are a gently rolling series of hillsides and valleys, while just a short distance away an interminable flatness seemingly extends forever. Clumps of trees, isolated pools of water, or the seasonally-changing crops provide textural relief. The wind and weather gently change the contour of the land, but undeniably a basic uniformity remains. The flatness of the prairies gives way to the undulating foothills of the mountains. This is the transition stage - an area of gently curving land forms, strongly three-dimensional but without the harshness, even violence, of the mountains. The foothills divide the mountains from the prairies, and yet they also create a continuity, flowing gradually and inclusively from one form into the other.

The mountains from a distance have a *sameness* about them as they are silhouetted against the sky. Approaching more closely, however, multiple forms become readily apparent. Cubes, octagons, cylinders, cones combine and integrate to form the barrier of the west. At close range they resemble sculpted forms that some anthropomorphic force has deliberately chiselled into shape. Each peak has its own individual characteristics, from jagged and precipitous to gently rounded; from the harsh rock-faces to the delicate alpine meadows. It is for this multiplicity of forms that the mountains are such a visually exciting and stimulating experience.

Each season has its own mood and sense of light and colour. The prairies awakening and fading, through brown, green, gold, white, with a rich variety of tones and subtle variations. The intense summer green of the trees in the foothills, changing to a magnificent flowing mosaic of yellows, oranges, browns and greens. In the winter the thin branches covered with brittle ice sculptures. The blues and greys of the mountains that emphasize their massiveness.

The sky in the West is unlike any other. The blue is undefinable in its depth and richness. In the mornings and evenings the sharp clarity of the horizon intensifies the continuously varying arrangements of colour and form. This is particularly true in the mountains, where the shape of each mountain is differently emphasized at various times of year. The seasons themselves manipulate and shape the forms.

Given the visual richness and variety of the West, it is not surprising that an extensive volume of written impressions has accumulated about the impact of the country upon its visitors. What is surprising is how nonchalant some early reactions were to this environment. For instance, Anthony Henday wrote on December 24th, 1754, "Travelled none: I found Buffalo lying dead a small distance from our tent. On a rising ground I had an extensive view of the *Arsinie Watchie* (Rocky Mountains) which will be the last this trip inland."[1] Henday was the first white man to see the Canadian Rockies and this is the only reference he makes to them.

The second account by a white man, Peter Fidler, in 1792, is not greatly different: "Awfully grand, stretching from ssw to wss by Compass, very much similar to dark rain like clouds rising up above the Horizon in a fine summer's evening."[2]

Sir Alexander Mackenzie, in 1793, was somewhat more descriptive: "At two in the afternoon the Rocky Mountains appeared in sight, with their summits covered with snow, bearing South-West by South: they formed a very agreeable object to every person in the canoe, as we attained the view of them much sooner than we expected."[3]

Some of the later visitors to the West were deeply impressed with the environment, however. In some ways the written word was more expressive than the early paintings and drawings, although occasionally a traveller mentioned that he wished "some painter had been there, to paint

Overleaf:
1. A.C. Leighton
Floe Lake, Marble Canyon
Water colour, 1930
14 5/8 x 18 1/2

what I so vainly try to describe."[4]

The Earl of Southesk, who toured the West from 1859 to 1860, dramatically described his reaction to his first sighting of the Rockies:

One solitary gleam of consolation enlivened this weary day - an unexpected, far-distant view of two grand peaks of the Rocky Mountains, over which a thunder-cloud cast a solemn, leaden shade. It was but an imperfect view, but so marvellous was the contrast between the damp, confined darkness of our track through the dripping fir-trees, and the sudden freedom of an open sky bounded only by magnificent mountain-forms, that for a moment I was quite overwhelmed. Then one of those strange tides of emotion that transcend both control and analysis, rushed through me from head to foot - I trembled all over - my limbs lost their strength, I could hardly sit on my horse. He, poor beast, did not share in his rider's excitement - as in a momentary fancy I thought he would - and seemed no happier than before; but, for my own part, all weariness vanished away, and I felt myself ready for any labours that might bring me nearer to so splendid a goal.[5]

Another relatively early tourist was W. H. Williams, who in 1881 was travelling with the Governor General of Canada, Lord Lorne. Williams most effectively conveys the beauty of this land:

Against this rich-coloured background, and in sharp relief rose the wild and rugged outlines of the mountain range, with its snow-clad peaks glittering in dazzling white as the sun lit up their gleaming slopes. Here were ruined towers and battlements and pyramids cut and polished in alabaster, as if some great city, realizing the grand dreams of the Apocalypse, had been hurled in

2. Marmaduke Matthews
Twin Mountain Peaks
Water colour, circa 1887-89
19 1/2 x 29 5/8

3. Belmore Browne
Under the Cliffs of Rundle
Oil, 1929
36 x 40

ruins upon the plains.

As I walked farther down the branch and reached the mill stream, I turned and looked up the deep narrow valley through which it runs, and here I saw one of the loveliest and most romantic of landscapes spread out before me. The deep canyon-like valley which opened in the foreground reached backward and upward away through the middle distance and into the background, where it was lost in the deep rich bronze of the foot hills, while above and beyond rose the great sharp mountain peaks wrapped in their pure spotless mantle of newly fallen snow. All along the valley were to be seen the brilliant autumnal tints on the frost-nipped foliage, in which light pea-green, lemon-chrome, straw colour, gold, orange, scarlet, and crimson were daintily blended, relieving the black green of the spruces, and the deep purplish bronze of the leafless brush and furze. Behind the great snow-capped peak on the right the sun was still shining, and its beams, streaming through the lofty wind-swept passes and narrow gorges among the mountain crests beyond, fell in bright belts and patches across the gorgeous medley of rich colours that adorned the shadowy slopes of the long deep valley.[6]

The first individuals visually to record the West were interested in documenting the land and its people, and also in portraying their own adventures. Probably the best known of these artists is Paul Kane, who made two trips to western Canada in the mid-19th century. The artists of this period were generally non-professionals, although the best of them were outstandingly capable, as their paintings clearly demonstrate. J.M. Alden, G. Brodie, G.A. Frost, and R.B. Nevitt, for instance, were all members of various expeditions. Each had a specific role to play, and painting was a secondary matter and a form of relaxation. The "expeditionary artists" for the most part were concerned with keeping a visual historic record of the voyage or trip, although the quality of their paintings often indicates an impressive understanding of the media and the subject matter.

The second group that can be recognized as such were the professional artists who visited western Canada following the completion of the Canadian Pacific Railway. Generally these were trained artists who were more interested in creating a personal interpretation of the western landscape than in compiling a visual documentary of an area or an event. Like the earlier travellers they were conscious of naturalistic representation and detail; where the two groups differ is that the professional artists could demonstrate a greater refinement and aesthetic sense in their painting. The professionals usually painted for a selling market or by commission - the C.P.R. itself hired a number of artists to record western Canada as part of a promotional scheme.

The next distinctive group can be termed "the first residents"- artists who were not from the West and whose artistic training was obtained in Europe, the United States, or eastern Canada, who chose to live permanently in this area rather than leave after one or more visits. Characteristically, the work of the first residents contrasts with that of the earlier professional artists by a stronger emphasis on expressing the mood or feeling of the landscape. The clear sense of naturalism is still unmistakable, but beyond this, a new dimension is evident. Artists such as W. J. Phillips vividly expressed the rich colour; Carl Rungius the monumentality and ruggedness; and A.C. Leighton the sense of space and sky of the West. These are not mere academic pictorial records, but paintings in which the energy of the country becomes as much a part of the creative concept as the image of the land. These are the first artists really to respond to the environment.

The final category comprises the artists who were born and raised in the West. With them the development of art in western Canada reached a new level, in that a particular western genre became recognizable for the first time. Their predominant influences were the precepts of the earlier resident artists, who themselves had already amassed a significant body of work; and above all, the intimate first-hand involvement with the country in which they spent their formative years. This is the distinctive attribute of the contemporary artists, from which has emerged a deep understanding and commitment to the land, and a determination to express it. The energy and dynamic quality so much a part of the western environment becomes an important element of interpretation. Painters such as Emily Carr, Illingworth Kerr, and Wynona Mulcaster, through the use of exaggerated and abstracted forms, vividly present images that convey much greater meaning than would be possible merely by straightforward representation of realistic scenes. On the other hand, artists such as Maxwell Bates, Otto Rogers, and Robert Sinclair minimize the elements of their work to illustrate the simplicity that can also be found in the western landscape.

The West is rich in subject matter and rich in

artistic heritage. The art that has developed in this tradition provides a unique portrayal of an environment that has its own qualities and moods.

Two passages express particularly well the thoroughness with which the land dominates awareness and sensitivity. Wallace Stegner conveyed the mood of the prairies in his book *Wolf Willow*:

The drama of this landscape is in the sky, pouring with light and always moving. The earth is passive. And yet the beauty I am struck by, both as present fact and as revived memory, is a fusion: this sky would not be so spectacular without this earth to change and glow and darken under it. And whatever the sky might do, however the earth is shaken or darkened, the Euclidean perfection abides. The very scale, the hugeness of simple forms, emphasizes stability. It is not hills and mountains which we should call eternal. Nature abhors an elevation as much as it abhors a vacuum; a hill is no sooner elevated than the forces of erosion begin tearing it down. These prairies are quiescent, close to static; looked at for any length of time, they begin to impose their awful perfection on the observer's mind. Eternity is a peneplain.[7]

Moira O'Neill, an Irish poetess who lived in Alberta from 1895 to 1902, described the impact of the mountains:

As you ride up and top this ridge, there bursts upon you quite suddenly the widest and most glorious view that can possibly be imagined. The ground at your feet falls away to a great distance, on your left by a steep slope covered with willows; there is a long, wide valley with stretches of willow and a gleam of water; then the ground rises and falls for miles in a succession of high, curving ridges, for all the world as if the earth had broken into billows like the sea. Some of these land-billows have exactly the curve and poise of a seawave before it breaks on the shore, but the cliffs they break against are the feet of the Rocky Mountains. Nothing could be more splendid than the immense chain of the Rockies seen from here. They rise and rise against the west, and from their very roots upwards to their shining crowns, you can follow the magnificent lines of their building - their vast bases, against which the billowing foothills dwindle to far-seen ripples, their towering heights and depths, the clefts and ledges piled with mountainous weights of snow, the jutting cliffs that watch at passing clouds, the great hollows that one guesses at from clear-cut shadows on the snow, and then the final glory of their sun-lit crests. So high and shining they are, they seem like some rampart to the world. If you look for a long while from here, you are seized with a fancy that all the earth is rolling towards the west, and there is nothing beyond the Rockies; they end the world and meet the sky.[8]

This book presents a number of artists who reacted to and painted the western landscape. All of the paintings are part of the collection of the Glenbow-Alberta Institute. The collection has largely grown out of a response to the West and the clearly recognized need to preserve its history. Some of the persons included here have far reaching reputations while others do not. *The Mountains and the Sky* is not a history of western Canadian art or of landscape art. It is a composite picture of how a number of exceptional artists have looked at and recorded an expressive and multiform environment.

4. I. H. Kerr
Barn with Stacks, Qu'Appelle Hills
Oil, 1929
18 7/8 x 24

1. The Expedition Artists

Overleaf:
5. R.B. Nevitt
Valley of the South Fork,
Old Man's River
Water colour, 1875
9 x 13

It was not until the middle of the nineteenth century that travellers began compiling a visual record of the environment of western Canada. The first artists who came to the area were intrigued both by the vast unexplored land and by the Indians, who - according to contemporary concepts - would provide a rich source of information. The land had been written about and described, but as such had never before been visually portrayed.

Some of the first artists were professional but for the most part the early travellers were what we would today call amateur. Many had had some training in artistic techniques but were not solely or primarily artists. Usually they came to the West for some purpose or function other than painting. For instance, George Brodie served as an officer on a British naval vessel, George Frost participated in the Western Union Telegraph expedition, and R.B. Nevitt was a doctor in the North West Mounted Police. However, this factor by no means negates the understanding the artists had for the western environment, or their desire, interest, and ability to express it in their paintings. Each in his own style and manner interpreted what he saw. The result is a priceless composite portrait of the face of the early West.

The paintings and drawings of the early artists were generally small in scale, ranging from three by five inches to fourteen by eighteen inches. The medium for these sketches would either be water colour, pencil, or pen, all of which were ideally suited for quick renderings and excellent portability. The early visitors had to travel with very little equipment, and generally were not in one location for any great length of time. It was essential to use material that could be unpacked and repacked with a minimum of difficulty.

The paintings or drawings done in the field would sometimes be finished works in themselves, or else would be used as the basis for oil paintings that would subsequently be made in the studio. When this was done, the paintings generally would take on a more formal and polished quality than the field sketches.

The early artists painted partly for their own enjoyment and desire, but also to compile a "formal" record of contemporary western life. The artists' paintings and drawings were frequently used to provide information for official reports or as sources of illustrations for publications. For instance, one of the artists in this chapter provided visual records to accompany government documents for the United States-Canadian boundary survey. Numerous other government papers were similarly illustrated. Often the same artists portrayed life in the West for popular magazines such as the *Canadian Illustrated News*. In this manner, although the original works may not have been widely seen, the reproductions did have a wide audience and impact. Thus the paintings achieved not only a high aesthetic standard, but must also be regarded as important historical documents.

Probably the earliest visual records of western Canada were made by Peter Rindisbacher. Rindisbacher settled at Red River, in present-day Manitoba, in 1821. He made numerous drawings and paintings of the North and of the area around Red River that graphically depict both the landscape and the native people.

After Rindisbacher, the first paintings of western Canada with significant artistic merit were made by Captain Henry Warre, who travelled west with Sir George Simpson in 1845. Although the Rocky Mountains had been written about prior to this time, Warre was the first person ever to portray them. Although there were a few other artists who painted the West around the early and middle 1800's, it was not until Paul Kane journeyed through western Canada between 1846 and 1848 that the richness of the country and the people was extensively recorded.

Paul Kane is unquestionably the dean of the early western Canadian artists. Kane was born in 1810 at Mallow, County Cork, Ireland, and emigrated to Canada with his family about 1819, settling in York, the present-day Toronto. After his schooling in Toronto, Kane did some portrait and landscape painting, in which he achieved indifferent success. He then spent five years travelling and painting in the United States before sailing for the Continent and England in 1841.

While in London he saw an exhibition of Indian paintings by George Catlin, who had travelled throughout the United States from 1830 to 1836 recording numerous Indian tribes. The paintings greatly impressed Kane, who decided that he too would paint the Indians of the western United States and Canada. As he later wrote in the preface to his book *Wanderings of an Artist* (published in 1858), "On my return to Canada from the continent of Europe, where I had passed nearly four years in studying my profession as a painter, I determined to devote whatever talents and proficiency I possessed to the painting of a series of pictures illustrative of the North American Indians and scenery."[1]

When Kane returned to Toronto in 1845, a

6. Paul Kane
Buffalo Reposing near Sturgeon Creek
Oil, no date
14 3/4 x 24 3/4

7. Earl of Dunmore
Souris River,
Water colour, circa 1862
9 1/4 x 13 3/4

8. Earl of Dunmore
Côteau des Prairies
Water colour, circa 1862
9 1/2 x 13 5/8

9. Paul Kane
The Encampment, Rocky Mountains
Oil, no date
13 5/8 x 20 1/8

10. James M. Alden
Kishinena Pass
Water colour, circa 1857-61
11 5/8 x 17 7/8

11. George S. Brodie
Sunset, Metlaskatla
Water colour, 1868
3 1/2 x 4 7/8

well travelled and competent artist, he immediately began preparations for the new project. His first trip, in 1845, was to the Mackinaw regions of the Great Lakes and Sault Ste. Marie, where he made a number of sketches of the Indians and the landscape. The following year he set off on a much more extensive two-year expedition, which took him across Canada to a point just south of present-day Portland, Oregon. During the trip he made about five hundred sketches and kept notes of his experiences. Upon his return to Toronto, Kane drew upon this immense wealth of preliminary work to prepare a number of large canvases. The sketches have a freshness and spontaneity to them that seem to capture the essence of the western Canadian environment; the finished oil paintings, on the other hand, are more academic and romanticized.

The composition of "The Encampment, Rocky Mountains" (Illustration No. 9) demonstrates Kane's technique of portraying the western landscape. Although the primary subject is the encampment, the landscape elements seem very deliberately built up of carefully structured pieces. While Kane portrays an image of space, there is no real sense either of the great depth or of the openess of the country. Similarly, Kane's mountains, while massive, are not painted with great definition or detail.

"Buffalo Reposing near Sturgeon Creek" (Illustration No. 6) has the same formal qualities as "The Encampment, Rocky Mountains". There is a strong presence and solidity not only to the animals but also to the landscape elements. A pronounced, almost heavy foreground brings strong initial contact with the scene. The painting then falls gently into the background, curving in such a manner as to repeat, horizontally, the painting format. Deep rich colours build up the land and also the textural sky. The result is a romantic representation of a western scene that was undoubtedly exaggerated from the freshness of the water colour.

Always in Kane's art the high degree of technical skill and the well trained hand of an expert painter are unmistakable. This artistic excellence, combined with the remarkable extent and variety of his work, gives Kane an important place in the history of Canadian painting. More than any other artist until the late nineteenth or early twentieth century, he is unsurpassed for the picture he created of the life and environment of western Canada.

Most of the other artists who travelled to western Canada at this time were Europeans who had come primarily to observe the country and its people. They were intrigued by the new lands they had learned of at second hand, and were keen to experience for themselves this largely unknown and unexplored territory. Predominantly they were "amateurs" - in the best sense of the word. As an aspect of the cultural milieu in which they lived, and through their cultural upbringing, most would have received art lessons, and would also have an intimate familiarity with the art of the day. This provided them with the technical skill and ability to interpret and paint what they saw. It was an interest which provided an important historical and artistic record of the early West.

One such man was Charles Adolphus Murray, Seventh Earl of Dunmore. Dunmore was a member of the Scots Fusilier Guards, and like many young officers from the British Isles, visited the United States to observe the Civil War. Dunmore travelled extensively throughout the United States and Canada; in later years he travelled to other parts of the world, including Africa and the Arctic.

During his travels in western Canada, Dunmore made numerous sketches which sensitively portray the western landscape. Like other artists of this period he worked primarily in water colour. His paintings of the Souris River (Illustration No. 7) and Côteau des Prairies (Illustration No. 8) are especially delicate and sensitive. Soft, carefully formed trees and bushes dot the landscape. The gentle gradation of colour expressly creates a sense of space and atmosphere. The carefully constructed perspective in which the landscape fades into the background creates a real sense of the infinity of the western countryside. The composition as a whole has the quality of completeness and unity, with a touch of elegance. A feeling of the English countryside can be sensed, even though the image is purely western Canadian.

Shortly after the middle of the nineteenth century a number of survey expeditions were made to western Canada. These expeditions established boundaries, charted waters, and in a very real sense helped to tame the West in order to facilitate settlement. The push of population was beginning, albeit on a relatively small scale, and it was imperative that physical markers and written and visual records be made. It was a general practice to include as part of an expedition an artist who would paint both the activities of the members as well as the country they passed through. Like Kane, the artists painted primarily in water colour and generally on a small scale.

One expedition that produced a number of excellent paintings was the United States-Canadian boundary survey of 1857-61. In the previous decade, one of the major boundary disputes between the United States and Great Britain concerned the present line between British Columbia and Washington, Idaho, and Montana. The United States claimed as far north as 50° 40', the present southern boundary of Alaska, while Great Britain claimed 40°, the present northern boundary of California. In 1846 a treaty was signed establishing the boundary at the forty-ninth parallel. However, it was not until ten years later that both countries established commissions to survey and mark the boundary's actual position. The survey itself presented exceptional difficulties:

The terrain was so difficult that the commissioners jointly decided they wouldn't try to clear or even mark the whole boundary. Here and there, instead, they would pin down astronomical points and cut a swath twenty feet wide for a mile on either side. They would do the same at every sizable stream, trail, settlement, or striking natural feature.

This was no job for tenderfeet, for the area was densely wooded, and in the higher reaches of the Cascades and Rockies perpetual snow covered the ground. Along the way someone struck gold. It was hard to keep the men on the job, and the wonder of it is that the survey was completed when it was, in 1861.[2]

The official artist of the United States commission was James M. Alden. Alden was born in 1834 and graduated from the Naval Academy at Annapolis. Prior to serving on the boundary survey, he had also participated as an artist on the United States hydrographic survey of the West Coast between 1854 and 1857. After completing his work on the boundary survey, Alden joined the Union Navy and continued with his painting during the Civil War, which he depicted in a number of water colours. After the War, Alden became secretary to Admiral David Dixon Porter, an association that continued until Porter's death. Alden died in 1922 in Florida, and was buried in Arlington National Cemetary.

During his service on the commission, Alden completed sixty-six water colours from the numerous coloured field sketches, which were undoubtedly scheduled for inclusion in the final report. Unfortunately, due to the debt incurred by the Civil War, the publication of the report was deemed too expensive, and consequently it never appeared.

In his paintings Alden generally employed a more topographical representation than, for instance, Paul Kane. An excellent example of Alden's approach is "Kishinena Pass" (Illustration No. 10), now called South Kootenay Pass, in the southern Rocky Mountains between Alberta and British Columbia. The careful articulation of shrubs, trees and the mountains in the background stands in contrast to Kane's smooth massive forms. Muted, almost muddy colours predominate. The variety of textures not only conveys the beauty of the area but creates the feeling of distance and depth. The carefully controlled use of perspective reinforces this sensation. A meandering stream gently flows out of the valley, thereby providing depth to the foreground. The sweep of the tree-covered mountains almost frames the roughly shaped peaks behind. The location of the camp in the lower right section creates a scale which enables the viewer to judge the immensity of the landscape. By making the camp an almost incidental detail, the sense of grandeur in the total scene in markedly increased. The overall effect is that the painting seems to curve and capture space.

During the nineteenth century, the Royal Navy was engaged in an extensive program of surveys to chart the seas along the north Pacific coast in an effort to reduce the number of shipwrecks in the area. One of the officers involved was George S. Brodie, who was aboard a hired Hudson's Bay Company vessel, the "Beaver". Brodie, who achieved the rank of Navigating Lieutenant, was not an official expedition artist, as Alden had been with the United States-Canadian boundary survey, but unquestionably the water colours he painted of the West Coast are of a very fine quality.

Brodie's paintings are small in size, ranging from about three by five inches to six by nine inches. Consequently, he seldom included a great amount of detail, although there are exceptions, such as the foreground in the painting "Mt. Baker, Washington Territory"(Illustration No. 12). Generally, Brodie used flat areas of paint to suggest forms, and did not blend one colour into another. As a result his paintings have a simplicity to them that captures the essence of the landscape. "Sunset, Metlaskatla" (Illustration No. 11) vividly shows this, with the few broad areas of paint forming

12. George S. Brodie
Mt. Baker, Washington Territory
Water colour, 1868
6 x 8 7/8

the water and defining the shape of the mountains in the background. The trees to the left are treated in a similar manner; Brodie does not concentrate on developing the fine details of each part of each tree.

The simplicity in expressing the landscape in Brodie's water colours gives a spontaneity to the scene. Brodie, like Kane, used water colours as studies for larger oil paintings, which were completed afterwards; as with Kane, his real understanding of the landscape is vividly expressed in the smaller pieces.

Brodie also had an excellent understanding of light. He used rich, luminous colours to emphasize graphically the intensity of the western sky and the brilliance of the countryside. In "Lowe Inlet" (Illustration No. 13), for instance, the clever use of grey creates a mood of light diffusing to the borders of the painting. The mountains and the water almost seem to radiate light instead of being emphasized by it.

Brodie did not attempt to achieve the effect of depth in his water colours. Usually there is water in the foreground, and then the mountains form the background for the composition. Even the sky seems to meet the mountains and not suggest further space. Brodie brings the landscape close to the viewer, but at the same time the viewer is not drawn visually into the painting.

Brodie, unlike Alden, did not strive for topographical interpretation, as this was not necessary for a primarily historical record. His fluid, almost relaxed style of painting is reminiscent of Dunmore, with a similar feeling of sophistication. Brodie clearly understood the principles of watercolour painting and the elements of landscape such as space and light, and how to interpret them with vivid effectiveness.

Another well known event of the nineteenth century was the Western Union Telegraph expedition, also known as the Collins Overland Telegraph, of 1865-67. This was an ambitious operation to establish a telegraph line from the United States to the west coast of British Columbia and Alaska, to Siberia, and then through Russia to India. The idea had been thought up by Perry McD. Collins, who at the time was a commercial agent in Siberia. Collins secured grants from Czar Alexander II and Queen Victoria to assist in the construction of the line, and in 1864 received $50,000 from the United States Congress. Work began enthusiastically in 1865 with a great deal of progress being made in the first season. The next year started off with the same sense of optimism

13. George S. Brodie
Lowe Inlet
Water colour, 1868
3 1/2 x 4 7/8

14. George S. Brodie
Needle Peak on the Portland Inlet
Water colour, 1868
3 1/4 x 4 7/8

15. George S. Brodie
Sunset, Lambert Channel, Vancouver Island
Water colour, circa 1868-70
5 x 7

16. George S. Brodie
McLaughlin Upper Lake
Water colour, circa 1868-70
5 1/2 x 9

and dedication. On July 27, 1866, however, Cyrus W. Field laid a cable across the Atlantic Ocean. This development virtually eliminated any chance of success for the Western Union venture, and in March of the following year all further work was stopped. News of this decision did not reach the expedition in Alaska until June of that year. The ambitious scheme to establish an inter-continental telegraph line then came to an abrupt end.

A number of artists went with the expedition, including Frederick Whymper, who was the official artist; Trautman Grob; and George A. Frost. Frost, who was born in Boston in 1843 and studied at the Royal Academy of Belgium, accompanied George Kennan of the Siberian detachment of the expedition. During this trip, Frost painted a number of water colours of the areas through which he travelled. He also provided illustrations for a book Kennan wrote to describe the trip, entitled *Tent Life in Siberia: A New Account of an Old Understanding, Adventures among the Koraks and Other Tribes in Kamchatka and Northern Asia*. Frost again accompanied Kennan to Siberia in 1885, almost twenty years later, on a trip sponsored by *Century Magazine*. During the trip Frost's physical and mental health collapsed, and it was a number of years before he recovered. However, he did provide several illustrations for Kennan's book *Siberia and the Exile System*, that described this journey to Russia.

Frost's paintings of the Western Union Telegraph expedition are quiet, almost idyllic landscapes. The composition clearly indicates that he had had professional training as well as unusual natural ability. Tight and carefully constructed, there is a definite foreground, middleground, and background in each piece. Usually trees frame the sides of the paintings. There is not the sense of spontaneity that is evident in Brodie's work; every part of Frost's paintings seems to be carefully arranged.

Frost was clearly influenced by European techniques. For instance, the trees he painted are "fluffy" and do not have the clear definition of a real tree. In his painting of Mt. Baker (Illustration No. 17), the trees on the right almost seem foreign to the western landscape. The same is true in "The Great Cañon" (Illustration No. 20) in which the trees seem a necessary part of the composition, but are not a realistic representation of trees found in that part of the world. Similarly, while he diminished and lightened the forms as they recede into the painting, he did not use the sky to reinforce the feeling of depth. His skies are usually

17. George A. Frost
Mt. Baker
Black ink wash, circa 1864-67
9 x 15

a flat colour without gradation or atmospheric change. Only occasionally did he introduce clouds.

Frost's paintings are generally representational statements of the environment, as seen by an artist trained in Europe. He did not try to formalize the landscape as Kane did in his finished oils, nor did he have the freshness that Brodie displayed in his water colours. Frost's paintings more closely resemble those of Alden, who also painted more-or-less strictly topographical representations of the landscape.

An expedition that changed the history of western Canada was the famous "March West" of the North West Mounted Police. The N.W.M.P. had been established in 1873 to bring law and order to the West and drive the American whiskey traders from the area. In May of the following year a large detachment set out from Dufferin, Manitoba, and

18. George A. Frost
Falls at Nicoamen, Thompson River, B.C.
Black ink wash, circa 1864-67
10 1/4 x 8

19. George A. Frost
Trutch's Bridge, Chapman's Bar, Fraser River
Black ink wash, circa 1864-67
9 3/8 x 12 1/8

20. George A. Frost
The Great Cañon
Black ink wash, circa 1864-67
10 1/2 x 15 7/8

21. George A. Frost
Suchalet Lake, B.C.
Black ink wash, circa 1864-67
8 1/2 x 14

22. George A. Frost
Cascade Range
Black ink wash, circa 1864-67
10 1/2 x 15 7/8

23. R.B. Nevitt
Second Crossing of the Souris
Water colour, 1874
7 x 9 15/16

after an extremely arduous trip, established their first western base at Fort Macleod, which was named after the leader of the march.

One of the officers and the Assistant Surgeon for the march was Richard Barrington Nevitt. Nevitt was born in Savannah, Georgia, on November 22, 1850. He fled the South when he became of military age at fourteen, just before General Sherman's army reached Atlanta in 1864. Nevitt felt that Canada provided his future opportunity.

Once in Canada, Nevitt resumed his interrupted education, eventually graduating from the University of Toronto with a B.A. in 1871. He then enrolled in Trinity Medical College to study medicine, but due to the expense of attending school and given the fact that he was not yet a qualified doctor, he was faced with the imperative need of finding employment. Consequently, he applied to the Mounted Police, and was appointed Assistant Surgeon in 1874. As the troops had already left Toronto for Dufferin, Nevitt departed immediately to catch up with them.

During Nevitt's period of service with the North West Mounted Police, which lasted from 1874 to 1878, he was extensively involved with his various medical duties. However, he did find time to draw and paint many aspects of western Canada. He painted a few water colours of the March West, although the most complete record was compiled by Henri Julien, who produced numerous sketches of the trek for the *Canadian Illustrated News*. The majority of the water colours by Nevitt are of the southern Alberta region through 1877.

Nevitt also wrote numerous extremely interesting letters describing his reaction to the West as well as his own activities. Shortly after arriving

24. R.B. Nevitt
Below Falls, Bow River
Water colour, 1876
9 7/8 x 13 7/8

at the site of Fort Macleod, Nevitt wrote:

This is a wild, wild region . . . . we have passed through a country dry, desolate and barren, a very Sahara. It was the northern portion of the Great American Desert; but now we have, fortunately, come into a country that shows, even in this late season, evidences of great fertility. We are just near the base of the Rocky Mountains; their snow-capped summits rise up to our left in jagged, rough peaks; the sun sinks behind them every night in one blaze of glory, making the most gorgeous sunsets that I have ever seen.[3]

Throughout his career in western Canada, Nevitt painted and drew numerous examples of the landscape, as well as events and people. His portfolio of works provides a unique visual insight into the history of Alberta from 1874 to 1877. Some of his water colours, such as the meeting of Colonel Macleod and Sitting Bull, and the encampment of Treaty No. 7, are the only known views of these events. A number of his drawings were also used in the *Canadian Illustrated News* in 1881.

Nevitt left the Mounted Police in 1878, and resumed his medical education in Toronto and London, England. He eventually became Dean of the Women's Medical College in Toronto, and one of the leading specialists in Gynecology and Obstetrics in the city. He maintained an active interest in the Sick Children's Hospital, St. Michael's Hospital, and the House of Providence, as well as his own private medical practice, until his death in 1928.

Nevitt's sketches, like those of other artists of this period, are relatively small in size. Nevitt often used both sides of a piece of paper, being as economical as possible with his scarce materials. In the interpretive sense, Nevitt unquestionably belongs in the same genre as the other painters, although certain differences should be noted between his work and that of several of the others. Unlike Kane or Frost, for instance, his paintings were not romantic in concept, and unlike Alden, were not primarily topographical. Nevitt more closely resembled Brodie and Dunmore in the freshness and honesty of his water colours; this is probably due to the fact that none of these artists had had professional training. There can be no question of Nevitt's competence, however. He was a man who strongly felt the impact of the western landscape and had the ability vividly to express it.

In all of Nevitt's paintings there is a strong sense of colour. The representation of "Lundbreck Falls" (Illustration No. 33) or the mountain landscape of "Below Falls, Bow River" (Illustration No. 24) vividly illustrate the rich and varied colour of the water, rocks and foliage. Blues, greens, reds, browns, and yellows all accent the various forms of the landscape.

Nevitt's works also capture the openess of the western terrain. In his rendering of the "Valley of the South Fork, Old Man's River" (Illustration No. 5), an infinite sense of distance is conveyed through the articulation of the clouds becoming less defined as they overlap the far-off mountains in the background. The clouds in "Rocky Mountains from Fort Calgary" (Illustration No. 27) almost form a ceiling for the distant mountains, but then curve upward, suggesting an undefined unlimited space. The flatness of the prairie is vividly suggested in "Old Man's River" (Illustration No.

25. R.B. Nevitt
Old Man's River
Water colour and pencil, 1876
6 7/8 x 9 13/16

26. R.B. Nevitt
Camp on the Prairies
Water colour, 1874
7 x 9 15/16

27. R.B. Nevitt
Rocky Mountains from Fort Calgary
Water colour and pencil, circa 1876
7 7/8 x 11 7/8

28. R.B. Nevitt
Old Man's River
Water colour, 1875
11 1/8 x 17 5/16

29. George S. Brodie
View from the Anchorage, Nanaimo
Water colour, 1868
3 1/4 x 4 7/8

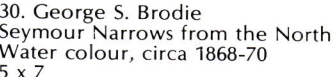

30. George S. Brodie
Seymour Narrows from the North
Water colour, circa 1868-70
5 x 7

31. George S. Brodie
Entrance to the Nass River
Water colour, 1868
3 1/4 x 4 7/8

32. George A. Frost
Scene near Nanaimo, Vancouver Island
Water colour, circa 1864-67
10 3/4 x 14 5/8

33. R.B. Nevitt
Lundbreck Falls
Water colour, 1875
10 7/8 x 9 5/8

34. R.B. Nevitt
Mountain Landscape
Water colour and pencil, circa 1875
6 7/16 x 9 9/16

35. R. B. Nevitt
The Porcupine Hills
Water colour, circa 1875
3 7/16 x 9 15/16

25) and "Camp on the Prairies" (Illustration No. 26). The horizontal plane of the ground continuously recedes, unbroken by hills or mountains. The sky is almost as flat but in a vertical direction. In "Mountain Landscape"(Illustration No. 34) the rock formations express what might be termed the "alternating quality of space" in the West - the tremendous concentration of form and detail at one point, and the almost total emptiness at another.

The six artists represented in this chapter illustrate the cross section of landscape art that developed prior to the 1880's in western Canada. All were rugged individuals who felt a desire to portray the West, although in most cases they were there primarily for reasons other than painting. Some of the artists gained reputations in their own day, while others have only won recognition in recent years. Each one looked at the western landscape as a source of visual information and found a need to record it on paper or canvas. The paintings range from romantic, almost idyllic, landscapes, such as Paul Kane's and George Frost's, to topographical representation like James Alden's, to spontaneous work like George Brodie's, Dunmore's, and R.B. Nevitt's.

Each of the artists helped in his own style to create a wide perspective of the many facets of the western landscape. With the coming of the railroad and the movement of people to the West, more and more artists journeyed to this land. It is to them we owe the real popularization of the western landscape.

2. The West Visited

In the early 1880's a few itinerant artists continued to travel through western Canada. However, it was with the completion of the Canadian Pacific Railway in 1885 that the full impact of the mountains and prairies as rich pictorial sources was made.

Prior to this time, travelling in the West was long and often difficult. The completion of the railway changed the situation tremendously; it was now possible for an artist to travel west, paint, and return home, usually to Toronto or Montreal, in one summer. This access of course facilitated a greater awareness and popularization of the western landscape, which in turn attracted an ever-increasing number of artists to this part of the country.

The C.P.R. contributed to the process through a promotional scheme of its own. William Van Horne, the President of the C.P.R., developed a program whereby artists were commissioned to do paintings of the mountains. The paintings were then used to advertize the railroad, and were displayed in various C.P.R. buildings. This program greatly expanded the knowledge of the West in other parts of Canada, and provided a financial means for the artists to pursue their work. Van Horne himself "was a tremendous art collector and connoisseur, as well as a painter."[1] Undoubtedly his decision to implement the program was influenced at least as much by his own interest in art as by any expectation of economic gain for the railway.

The annual exhibitions of the Royal Canadian Academy and other exhibitions in many cities in Canada and United States also contributed to an awareness of the western landscape. Magazines as well provided an outlet for paintings, and a further popularization of the genre.

While the first artists to travel in western Canada were largely interested in historical and topographical representation, the artists of the 1880's and later were more interested in the landscape for its own sake. They were professional artists who concentrated on painting for their livelihood. Their paintings were stronger visual statements than those of the earlier artists. The interpretation was no longer strictly realistic, but had a sense of naturalism, a feeling for the landscape elements. An emotional reaction and response to the landscape was increasingly recognizable. Landscape art became more than just a topographical record. The true *artistic* expression of the West actually began in the 1880's.

In addition to the change of emphasis and interpretation, a further aspect which distinguished the "railway artists" from their predecessors was that they were much more involved in the artistic life of the East than the earlier artists had been. One such person was Arthur P. Coleman, a distinguished geologist and a prolific painter. Born in Lachute, Lower Canada, on April 4, 1852, Coleman attended Victoria University in Cobourg, Ontario, receiving a B.A. in 1876 and an M.A. in 1880. He continued his education at Breslau University in Germany, where he attained a Ph.D degree in 1881. He taught geology at a number of universities, including Victoria University, the School of Practical Science, Toronto, and the University of Toronto, where he was Dean of the Faculty of Arts from 1919 to 1922. As well as receiving numerous honorary degrees, Coleman was the author of *The Canadian Rockies*, *Ice Ages, Recent and Modern*, and a co-author of *Elementary Geology*.

Coleman's primary geological interest was glaciers, and he travelled throughout the world gathering data and accumulating pictorial records of them. His travels took him to such far-reaching places as Kilimanjaro, Spitzbergen, the Andes, and the Rockies. In both 1883 and 1884, Coleman came west and painted scenes of the mountains, some of which were exhibited at the Royal Canadian Academy. Coleman made other trips to the Rockies, including two unsuccessful attempts to climb Mt. Robson in 1907 and again in 1908.

Coleman's painting of Mt. Robson (Illustration No. 37), was probably done on one of these climbing expeditions. The details of the mountain are largely obscured by mist, with the jagged top being the only clearly defined feature. The colours help create a slightly eerie atmosphere, with the soft green foreground giving way to blue-grey mist. The small areas of brown water-colour highlight the mountain, and provide definition for it. Through his minimal use of middleground, Coleman has emphasized two distinct qualities of the landscape: the lush foreground, and the crisp mountain peak. The sense of depth between the two is vividly represented.

A railway artist who not only painted landscapes of the West but also worked on the building of the railway in the mountains was Herbert B. Lewis. Very little is known of Lewis other than that he was born in Llandilo, South Wales, and that after leaving the C.P.R. he moved on to California. He is, however, mentioned in P. Turner Bone's contemporary account of the building of the C.P.R., *When the Steel Went Through*. Bone,

Overleaf:
36. F.M. Bell-Smith
Glacier Stream, Selkirks, B.C.
Oil, no date
15 x 21 1/4

37. Arthur P. Coleman
Mt. Robson
Water colour, no date
5 7/8 x 3 3/4

38. Herbert B. Lewis
Mountain Range
Water colour, 1886
9 x 12 1/2

39. Herbert B. Lewis
Landscape
Water colour, 1886
12 3/8 x 9

40. Herbert B. Lewis
Mountain Landscape near Golden, B.C.
Water colour, 1886
9 x 12 1/2

41. Herbert B. Lewis
Landscape
Water colour, no date
12 3/8 x 9

Lewis, and a few others made sketches and water colours of their work and the environment. "There were, however, no kodaks in those days with which to take snapshots. There were a few itinerant photographers who took photos here and there along the route of the railway; and one could buy photos of the scenes one particularly wanted. So we developed a taste for sketching; and it was our custom when we paid a visit to a neighbouring engineer's camp on a Sunday, to take our portfolio of sketches with us to submit them for inspection and criticism. This criticizing of each other's work proved most helpful."[2]

Lewis's four monochromatic water colours show a highly stylized treatment of the mountains. The trees have very little definition, and actually appear as silhouettes rather than three-dimensional forms. In the background the trees become bands of vertical brush strokes. Lewis also emphasized the shapes and rhythm of the mountains; in "Mountain Range" (Illustration No. 38), for example, a strong curving line clearly breaks the foreground from the peaks in the background, and also provides a frame for the jagged mountains.

In "Mountain Landscape near Golden, B.C." (Illustration No. 40) Lewis once again used the curve of the mountains to define both the foreground and the background. The stylization of the landscape can also be seen in the glacier, which seems to lie on the mountains rather than form an integral part of the structure. In Lewis's water colours the clear definition given each compositional component makes them all seem individualized and separate, rather than interrelated as one overall scene.

Lewis had less professional training than any of the other painters discussed in this chapter, and also had less opportunity for contact with other artists. This is immediately apparent in his work, although it in no way constitutes a deficiency or shortcoming. The freshness of his painting is immensely attractive, and in many ways compares favourably with the more sophisticated approach of the professional artists.

The year 1887 brought four outstanding landscape artists to the West. These were Lucius R.

42. Lucius R. O'Brien
Puget Sound
Water colour, 1887
9 5/8 x 16 1/2

O'Brien, T. Mower Martin, Marmaduke Matthews, and F. M. Bell-Smith. Each of the four continued to visit and paint western Canada for varying periods of time.

Lucius R. O'Brien was born in 1832 at Shanty Bay, Ontario, and attended Upper Canada College, Toronto. In 1847 he entered an architect's office and later studied and practised as a civil engineer. He did not have any formal art training, although undoubtedly he was involved with art during his architectural studies.

Although he did not turn to painting until 1872, O'Brien was to have a great impact on the development of art in Canada. He was a member of the Ontario Society of Artists, and became president of the Society in 1879. When the Governor General of Canada, the Marquis of Lorne, put forth the suggestion for the formation of a Royal Canadian Academy, O'Brien, as president of the Ontario Society, met with him to discuss the situation. Shortly afterwards permission was granted by the government to form a new society, the Royal Canadian Academy.

Membership was drawn from both the Ontario Society of Artists and the Art Association of Montreal, with nineteen original members and twenty-four associate members. O'Brien was elected the first president of the R.C.A., a post he was to hold until 1890.

In addition to his involvement in the Royal Canadian Academy, O'Brien also developed and acted as editor of *Picturesque Canada*. For this double volume, which was published in 1882, O'Brien commissioned a large number of artists to paint scenes of all parts of the country. The paintings were then transferred into woodcuts, which were used for printing.

Picturesque Canada had a significant effect on the art scene of the 1880's. Not all comment was positive, but generally the reception was favourable: "Canadians grumbled about the high-handed way in which O'Brien produced illustrations for his volumes, and in fact some artists whom he had ignored made an attempt to produce a rival volume. Yet the ambitious *Picturesque Canada* made available to public and artists alike the first great series of locally produced Canadian scenes, and it came at a time when nationalism was being aroused on all sides."[3]

With the advent of the Royal Canadian Academy and its annual exhibitions; a popular book such as *Picturesque Canada*; exhibitions held at other galleries; and finally with William Van Horne's promotional scheme, the western landscape was receiving a great deal of exposure and was attracting more and more artists to the West to paint.

Despite the fact that O'Brien did not begin painting seriously until he was forty years old, he quickly achieved an outstanding level of success. He was commissioned to paint two works of Quebec for Queen Victoria, and the Marquis of Lorne was also his patron. O'Brien continued to paint various Canadian scenes of excellent quality until his death in 1889.

William Colgate wrote of O'Brien's paintings, "Essentially a water colourist, he painted in a limpid, flowing style, and was technically an expert in his craft; but his pictures are often destitute of imagination and invention, since they are to a noticeable degree exact copies of nature, and subject as they were to his training as an engineer, valuable chiefly for their topographical interest."[4]

Colgate's statement is only partially true. In the painting "Puget Sound", for instance, (Illustration No. 42) O'Brien's use of texture is obvious. He has built up a complexity of colour to indicate a continuous form across the near foreground. The lushness of the foliage almost becomes a dense wall over which the scene recedes into a relatively open, light background, thereby creating a counterbalancing effect. The outline of the foliage is echoed by the mountains to provide a horizontal rhythm to the painting. The mountains are not represented by detailing, but are built up of areas of colour each creating its own forms. The sky, in contrast to the harsh green of the foliage, is a definite and soft blue. Clearly the painting is only topographical in the placement of forms. In terms of the overall work, O'Brien has freely interpreted the essence of the landscape.

T. Mower Martin was born on October 5, 1838, in London, England. His father was acting-treasurer of the Inner Temple in London, and consequently the ancient cloister of that historic building was his playground. Through contact with influential people he developed an interest in art and literature, and regularly visited the Royal Academy. Although Martin was educated for the East India Company and sent to a military college at Enfield, he decided to turn to painting as his profession.

In 1862, Martin and his bride came to Canada and settled at Muskoka. They spent their first year there, but due to the cold they went to Toronto, where Martin continued successfully with his painting. Like O'Brien, he was a charter member of the Ontario Society of Artists and the Royal Canadian Academy, and exerted a considerable influence on

43. T. Mower Martin
Landscape with Boat
Water colour, 1887
20 1/2 x 13 1/4

44. T. Mower Martin,
Landscape
Water colour, 1887
20 3/4 x 13 1/8

45. Marmaduke Matthews
Mt. Burgess
Water colour, circa 1887-89
21 1/4 x 30

46. T. Mower Martin
Train in the Mountains
Oil, no date
36 x 54 1/4

36. F. M. Bell-Smith
Glacier Stream, Selkirks, B.C.
Oil, no date
15 x 21 1/4

47. Marmaduke Matthews
Monarch of the Selkirks
Water colour, circa 1887-89
14 5/8 x 19 7/8

48. Marmaduke Matthews
Valley of the North Kicking Horse, B.C.
Water colour, circa 1887-89
20 1/4 x 30

49. Marmaduke Matthews
Solitary Pine
Water colour, circa 1887-89
13 3/4 x 20

50. John Hammond
The Three Sisters
Oil, circa 1895
48 x 72

Near right:
52. Theodore J. Richardson
Scene in British Columbia
Water colour, no date
11 x 17 5/8

Far right:
53. Cleveland Rockwell
Grenville Channel, B.C.
Water colour, 1884
14 x 20

51. F.M. Bell-Smith
Morning, Lake Louise
Water colour, 1909
17 1/2 x 23 3/8

54. Cleveland Rockwell
Banff Springs Hotel
Water colour, 1904
14 7/8 x 21

55. Leonard M. Davis
Harvesting, Nobleford
Oil, 1918
36 x 54

56. T. Mower Martin
Trial Island from near Victoria
Oil, 1902
13 x 19 1/2

the early Canadian art scene. For a period of time he taught at the Central Ontario School of Art. He lived in Toronto until his death in 1934.

Martin had a deep interest in the land. He made numerous trips across Canada, some of which were sponsored by the Canadian Pacific Railway. The C.P.R. used a number of his paintings of the mountains for promotional purposes. In 1907, Adam and Charles Black of London published *Canada*, a book with text by William Wilfred Campbell and seventy-five illustrations by Martin. The book itself is almost an emotional plea for respect for the land, an attempt "to describe the great natural features of the land in its broader characteristics . . . for which the region is specially famous . . . . The vastness, the grandeur of the scenery, the miles upon miles of country over which [the visitor] is being rapidly whirled, while the ever-varying panorama materializes and dissolves as he passes, must be a continual source of astonishment and admiration. And though he may have seen the beauty and grandeur of the great lakes, he is scarcely prepared for the scene which awaits him after he passes the wide prairies, through seas of waving grass, and the glorious vision of the Rocky Mountains arises like a vast new dream conjured up by Dante, or touched by the masterhand of that magician, Turner."[5]

Campbell's text deals with Canada proceeding from the Maritimes westward, with Martin's paintings visually complementing the written word. His paintings show a variety of typical scenes of Canada. The book was very well received in its day.

Martin worked in both oil and water colour. Although on his trips west he was primarily commissioned to paint landscapes, he also did numerous paintings of Indians and their villages. He painted both on location and in the studio.

"Train in the Mountains" (Illustration No. 46) is an excellent example of Martin's oil paintings. He does not include a high degree of detail, but instead concentrates on building up very plastic forms, such as the highly moulded rocks in the foreground. The mountains in the background are carefully and strongly built up with wide heavy brushstrokes. Martin does not itemize every detail; rather, he vividly represents the essence and power of the mountains. The clouds are softly rounded and dynamically constructed - the manipulating of the forms, the careful brushwork, and the integration and use of colour all create a sensation of movement. The train and tracks give depth to the foreground of the painting, but almost seem incidental except to provide a sense of scale. The general colours seem muted in comparison to the rich natural hues of the mountains.

Martin's use of earth-coloured tonality can also be seen in two other oil paintings, "Trial Island from near Victoria" (Illustration No. 56) and "Arrow Lakes, B.C." (Illustration No. 60). In both of these

57. T. Mower Martin
At Howe Sound
near Vancouver, B.C.
Water colour, no date
10 1/4 x 21 3/4

58. T. Mower Martin
Rocky Mountains
Water colour, no date
13 1/2 x 26

59. T. Mower Martin
The Bow River
from the Banff Hotel
Water colour, no date
9 7/8 x 17 3/8

60. T. Mower Martin
Arrow Lakes, B.C.
Oil, no date
14 x 22

2. Marmaduke Matthews
Twin Mountain Peaks
Water colour, circa 1887-89
19 1/2 x 29 5/8

61. Marmaduke Matthews
South Bank of the Bow River near Laggan
Water colour, circa 1887-89
19 3/4 x 29 3/4

paintings browns, mauves, and deep blues predominate. Rich vibrant colours are noticeably absent. Once again Martin does not provide a great amount of detailing in expressing the landscape elements. Broad areas of paint are used to build up components such as the mountains in "Arrow Lakes, B.C.". A high degree of surface texture is achieved by manipulating the paint with the brush and a palette knife; this gives an added dimension to the painting, so that the surface conveys some of the rugged textural quality of the forms in the landscape. The artist is not only representing a scene but expressing his medium.

Unlike the oil paintings, Martin's water colours obviously do not have this feeling of surface texture. In neither the oil paintings nor the water colours does Martin include a high sense of detail. Instead there is a definite naturalness in the composition and an understanding of each scene. He does of course give more definition to details such as the rocks and trees in the foreground of his paintings.

Martin's water colours have richer tones than the oil paintings, but still could not be described as intense. There is a subtlety in the water colours which contrasts to the dynamic quality of the oil paintings. The rocks and the mountains are all carefully built up. Delicate small areas of colour are used to define the mountains, thereby giving a plasticity to the various shapes. The trees have the same feeling of having been very delicately arranged in expressive forms.

All Martin's paintings, both in oil and water colour, are generally tight, intense views of the landscape. Their characteristic features are a gently receding foreground that goes to the foot of the mountains, and a gradual transition from the picture frame to the vertical background to provide a dynamic and tightly woven composition. Martin's paintings are invariably powerful and impressive.

A third artist who came west in the year 1887 was Marmaduke Matthews. Matthews was born in 1837 at Barchester, Warwickshire, England. After studying at Cowley Diocesan School, Oxford, under T. M. Richardson, he emigrated to Canada in 1860, settling in Toronto. Except for the years 1865-69, when he was in New York, he continued to live in Toronto until his death in 1913.

Matthews was a founding member of the Ontario Society of Artists, and held various positions in that organization from 1875 to 1897. He was also a charter member of the Royal Canadian Academy.

According to recollections by his daughters, Matthews made only two trips west, one in 1887 at the request of the C.P.R., to record the scenery through the Kicking Horse Pass, and the second in 1889, when he travelled to the Coast where he painted Nanaimo. "Miss Matthews well remembers her father's thrilling account of riding on the cow-catcher of the engine through this rugged country in order to make sketches."[6]

Matthews's water colours generally have a looseness and freshness to them. The foliage in the foreground is built up in some detail using opaque layers of paint. Highlights are placed in the foliage by small dabs of white paint, which provide an accent but do not give a high degree of realism. In contrast to the opacity of the foreground, the mountains in the background seem translucent. The paint is applied very thinly to suggest the shapes of the mountains but not to define any specific characteristics. The paint appears to be loosely layered on the surface of the paper, and while it has a three-dimensional quality, it is not in any way plastic. The paintings almost seem divided into foreground and background by the contrasting shapes in each area, although a continuity is nevertheless maintained. The result is a highly romantic interpretation of the mountains, rather than a realistic representation. Matthews does not clearly and precisely define each element in his paintings, but instead presents a feeling for the landscape as a total unit.

The fourth artist to travel west in 1887, Frederick M. Bell-Smith, was born in London, England, in 1846, the son of a portrait painter. As well as studying under his father, Bell-Smith studied with Alexander Harrison at the South Kensington Art School in London. He also studied at the Académie Colarossé in Paris in 1891. In 1866 he emigrated with his father to Canada and settled in Montreal. He worked as a photographer in Montreal and later in Hamilton.

In 1881 Bell-Smith turned to teaching art. He was appointed Director of Fine Arts, Alma College, St. Thomas, Ontario, a post he held until 1901. Concurrent with this position, Bell-Smith was Director of Fine Arts of the Public Schools, London, Ontario, from 1882 to 1888, and Principal of the western branch of the Toronto Art School from 1888 to 1890. After 1890 he worked primarily as a painter in Toronto.

Bell-Smith did numerous magazine and newspaper illustrations throughout his career for publications such as the *Canadian Illustrated News* and *Picturesque Canada*. He also compiled an illustrated record for the Governor General's tour of south-western Ontario in 1872. He was a found-

62. Marmaduke Matthews
Puffing Billy
Water colour, no date
7 5/8 x 10

ing member of the Society of Canadian Artists in 1867, and the Ontario Society of Artists in 1872. He was elected an associate of the Royal Canadian Academy in 1880 and a full member in 1886.

Bell-Smith made several trips to western Canada, and gained a certain reputation for his paintings of the mountains. After his first trip in 1887 he was interviewed by the Winnipeg *Free Press*. "Mr. F.M. Bell-Smith of the Royal Canadian Academy of Artists has just returned from a two month's sketching tour in the Rockies. He has brought back with him studies enough to make work for him for two or three years. Tourists who passed through the mountains while he was there have given him orders for $3,000 worth of pictures to be elaborated from the sketches which they saw. In making his selections for sketches Mr. Bell-Smith took only striking effects or studies of details to enable him to give his works faithful elaboration. He says he has not attempted to idealize at all, but simply to copy nature truly."[7]

Travel in the West had become relatively easier, but still was not without excitement. "They worked hard and had only one adventure," continued the *Free Press*, referring to his 1887 trip, "which fell to the lot of Mr. Bell-Smith. He was sitting sketching one day when a large bear passed within one hundred feet of him. It made no attempt to molest him however, but slowly trotted off into some bushes. He did not give it an opportunity to reflect upon the capital meal left untasted, but lit out for home."[8]

Three paintings aptly show the typical qualities of Bell-Smith's work - the richness of colour and the crispness of form. "Glacier Stream, Selkirks, B.C." (Illustration No. 36) is a strong example. The stream tumbling over the debris of logs and spreading across the bottom pulls the painting to the viewer. The surface texture of the paint reinforces the feeling of rapid motion. The rocks flanking the stream are very moulded in their shape, and provide a counterbalance to the visual texture of the water. A band of green curves across the painting framing the picturesque and rugged mountains. The mountains themselves are built up by a massive juxtaposition of various rock shapes and snow patches. The rich colours of all the forms convey a sense of realism even though the forms are not painted in minute detail.

Another painting by Bell-Smith which has a visual realism is "Mt. Baker from Oak Bay, Victoria, B.C."(Illustration No. 63). The rugged, carefully defined rocks contrast with the smooth mirror surface of the water. The colours give a distinct

vibrancy to the scene. Bell-Smith's gentle gradation of the atmosphere provides a strong sense of depth. Mt. Baker is only faintly represented but the naturalness is readily apparent.

"Morning, Lake Louise" (Illustration No. 51) has the same rich colours as the other two paintings. However, by using water colours instead of oils, there is not the crispness of the landscape elements. The enclosure of mountains rising from the lake and the effect of light on the peaks accurately portray the mood of this area of the Rockies. The camp scene on the left side provides a human proportion to the composition. The mountains, particularly those at the back, have a solidity about them which is characteristic of the Bell-Smith mountain paintings.

Lucius O'Brien, T. Mower Martin, Marmaduke Matthews, and F. M. Bell-Smith initially travelled to western Canada at the same time under the sponsorship of the C.P.R. Through their paintings these four artists greatly stimulated an interest and appreciation for the western landscape. Each in his own style vividly and realistically understood the beauty of the environment. Although earlier artists had recorded the West, it was not until this time that a true popularization was realized.

For a number of years the C.P.R. continued to sponsor artists to travel through western Canada to provide visual material for promotional purposes. One of the foremost artists who travelled west in the 1890's under the auspices of the railway was John Hammond.

Born in Montreal in 1843, Hammond at an early age wished to become an artist: "Hammond started to work when he was nine years old, in a marble mill. When he was eleven he had made up his mind to be an artist and he has been steadfast to his purpose ever since."[9] Despite this early interest, Hammond did not take formal art training, although he studied with a number of masters.

Hammond had an adventurous life. In 1886 he joined the army and participated in the campaign against the Fenian rebels. After his discharge, he and his brother left for New Zealand to find their fortunes searching for gold. Two and a half years later, in 1870, Hammond returned to Canada. However, his travelling days were far from over. He joined the first Transcontinental Survey, possibly as a photographer's assistant, and reached Yellowhead Pass. After the survey he was employed by William Notman photographers in Montreal.

In the next few years Hammond began to turn more and more to painting, including a number of commissioned portraits. In 1885 he left for Europe for a period of about two years. During this time he met and studied with Whistler and Charles Storm de Gravesend in Holland, and François Millet in the Barbizon district in France. He also stayed for a time in Italy.

Hammond also travelled extensively between

63. F.M. Bell-Smith
Mt. Baker from Oak Bay,
Victoria, B.C.
Oil, no date
11 x 17 1/2

1889 and 1901 in Europe, America, China, and Japan. He was in Canton in 1900 during the Boxer Rebellion, where he reportedly commented, "I was pursued by a rabble of Chinamen . . . got to my ship safely and for the next days . . . was content to stay on board and study Canton, and the Chinese, from the deck."[10]

Hammond began a distinguished educational career in 1892 when he became Director of Owen's Art Institution, St. John. In 1893 he went to Mount Allison Ladies College in Sackville, and in 1907 was appointed Director of the School of Art at Mount Allison College, a post he held until his retirement in 1919. He continued to live in Sackville until his death in 1939.

Hammond participated in numerous exhibitions, including the Paris Salon Exhibition, 1886; the National Gallery, Washington, 1887; the Pan-American Exhibition, Buffalo, 1901; and the Louisianna Purchase Exhibition, St. Louis, 1904. He was elected an associate of the Royal Canadian Academy in 1890 and a full member in 1893, and participated in the R.C.A. annual exhibitions from 1901 to 1935. He was also an early member of the Ontario Society of Artists.

Hammond was commissioned by the C.P.R. to do several paintings of western Canada. "The Three Sisters" (Illustration No. 50), a large canvas which hung in the Palliser Hotel in Calgary for a number of years, is an excellent example. The painting itself is a majestic representation of three very prominent and well known peaks. In the picture Hammond has conveyed an extraordinary sense of space by the pronounced breaking away of the foreground. The rhythm of the mountains sloping to the left forces the space back into infinity. This feeling of tremendous area is further reinforced by the clouds that overlap the far right mountain peak. The small stream of smoke on the left side, possibly from a train, dramatically emphasizes the majestic quality of the mountains. The miniscule proportions of the smoke almost seem out of scale to the landscape. The individual forms within the painting are vividly built up and then gently pulled together by the use of colour. The total painting thus becomes an integral unit that realistically and powerfully presents the mountain scene.

"Coldstream Ranch" (Illustration No. 64) was commissioned by William Van Horne in 1896 as a presentation gift to Lady Aberdeen, the wife of the Governor General of Canada. The ranch, near Vernon, British Columbia, was owned by Lord and Lady Aberdeen. The painting was taken

64. John Hammond
Coldstream Ranch
Oil, 1896
18 1/8 x 30

back to Scotland by them and hung in Haddo House until it was returned to Canada in the early 1960's.

Once again Hammond has vividly expressed a sense of space in his composition. The road leading into the painting is dramatically contained by large trees that emphasize a sense of depth. The shadow across the foreground gently frames the bottom part of the scene. The hills in the background and the clouds have an expressionistic effect to them, and are not reproduced in tight detail. The energy of these environmental elements conveys a sense of empathy for the land - the painting is not merely a strict representation. This understanding of the landscape constitutes a marked difference from the paintings done by the early artists who visited western Canada.

Not all the artists who travelled through the West in the late nineteenth century came under the auspices of the C.P.R. One such "independent" artist was Edward Roper, an Englishman who travelled across Canada in 1887. Roper had previously travelled extensively in other parts of the world, and was anxious to visit and record scenes of the great Canadian West.

During his journey from Quebec to Victoria, Roper not only painted numerous illustrations of the landscape and the Indians, but also pursued his interests as a naturalist. In his travels he examined the flora and fauna of the region, and collected samples of the flowers, butterflies, beetles, and moths, which he took back to England. Roper wrote a book about his Canadian trip, which he illustrated with forty-four of his own sketches. The book, entitled *By Track and Trail, a Journey Through Canada with Numerous Original Sketches by the Author*, was published in London in 1891.

65. John Hammond
Canadian Rockies, Banff
Oil, 1900
5 1/2 x 8 1/2

"Roper . . . was particularly interested in the mountains. The composition of his picture is well arranged, - impressive mountains often snow-capped, dominate the background to which converge lower slopes covered with foliage. The foreground usually comprises considerable detail, - trees take on their individual characteristics, a small mountain stream bubbles over the boulders, a lake nestles in a natural basin, or along the Pacific Coast one looks across large expanses of water to the hazy mountains in the distance."[11]

Roper's small sketch "Mt. Field and Mt. Stephen" (Illustration No. 66) shows many of these characteristics. The mountains are massive in their formation, with gently rolling hills forming a transition to the lush foreground. A great amount of detail is included in the trees and bushes of the foreground, with particular attention given to the leaves on the bush at the picture plane. The scene is held together very tightly, and gives an

66. Edward Roper
Mt. Field and Mt. Stephen
Tempera, circa 1887
5 x 8 3/4

67. Cleveland Rockwell
The Inland Passage, B.C.
Water colour, 1884
13 7/8 x 19 7/8

almost photographically realistic view. Roper sometimes added a foreign element to his composition, such as the train on the left of the painting. While this detail adds a sense of scale, it somehow seems to detract from a central theme of the work.

In addition to the English artists travelling through western Canada, a number of Americans also came to paint the landscape. One of these was Theodore J. Richardson, who made eighteen trips to Alaska between 1884 and his death in 1914. During these visits he also painted numerous studies of British Columbia. Richardson was born in Minnesota in 1855. He spent his life there teaching drawing and geometry, eventually becoming Supervisor of Industrial Drawing for the Public School System in Minneapolis.

Richardson worked primarily in water colour, although in his later years he concentrated more and more on oil. His painting "Scene in British Columbia" (Illustration No. 52) presents a very peaceful, almost idyllic view of the landscape. Very little articulation is used to build up the forms. Instead, Richardson uses loose brushstrokes and relatively broad bands of colour. The river meanders towards the gently rolling hills of the background from which the one peak rises. Richardson does not provide a great amount of detail to build up the mountain.

Cleveland Rockwell was an artist who came to landscape painting from a background as a specialist in topography. He was born in 1837 in Youngstown, Ohio; very little is known of his early years, except that he attended New York University, and undoubtedly took some courses in engineering. In 1856 he was appointed to the United States Coast Survey and until the Civil War was posted in the War Department for topographical work. His maps were considered among the finest defense maps produced during the War, and were extensively used during Sherman's "March to the Sea". Largely due to his topographical ability he was appointed Captain of Engineers.

After the Civil War, Rockwell made a short mapping tour of South America before being appointed as Chief of the United States Geodesic Survey in the Northwest in 1868. He settled in Portland, which became the base of his surveys of California, Oregon, British Columbia, and Alaska. Most of his work was concentrated on the Columbia River, although he did make numerous trips elsewhere. He visited Banff in 1904. The numerous sketches made on his mapping expeditions became the basis for later more colourful oil and water-colour paintings.

Rockwell exhibited extensively in San Francisco and also in Portland. He was instrumental in founding the Portland Art Club. He wrote and illustrated articles for *Pacific Coast Pilot*, and some of his paintings were reproduced in *Pacific Monthly* and *West Shore*. He died in 1907.

Rockwell's paintings have a high sense of realism. "He did not seek to present nature as a clash of the elements. He was not a mood painter and was not influenced by such work. Nothing of the mystical or allegorical crept into his work.... Other painters may have grappled with the problem of how to present nature, but for Cleveland Rockwell there was only one way. He painted what he knew."[12]

The topographical influence in Rockwell's paintings is unmistakable, and to a certain degree is reminiscent of the work of J. M. Alden. In Grenville Channel, B.C.", for instance, (Illustration No. 53), each mountain, tree, and even each rock on the beach is precisely defined and shaped. In a sense it is almost a photographic image that is being shown. Rockwell did not try to generalize or romanticize. His intention was faithfully to record what he saw and knew.

The same is true of "The Inland Passage B.C." (Illustration No. 67). While this is a carefully constructed painting, one does not feel that the artist is adding or subtracting anything from the scene in order to present a more pleasant composition.

Eleven years later, when Rockwell painted "Harrison Lake, B.C." (Illustration No. 69), he had not lost any of his interest in meticulous accuracy. Because of their high degree of realism, his paintings do not appear superficial in any respect. There is a sense of life and authenticity in each scene. Rockwell does not use the rich, vibrant colours found in Bell-Smith's paintings, for example. Instead they are soft and almost subdued, but at the same time faithful to the actual colouring of each landscape.

In 1904, just three years before his death, Rockwell visited Banff and painted a number of water colours of that area. "Banff Springs Hotel" (Illustration No. 54) was one of the paintings done on this trip. The foreground, characteristically, has a great sense of detailing. The composition is bisected by the meandering road along which an Indian is walking towards the viewer. The figure serves to establish the proportion of the landscape. The curve of the mountain sweeps down joining the line of the road. This conver-

68. Cleveland Rockwell
Glacier on Frederick Sound, Alaska
Water colour, 1884
13 3/4 x 19 3/4

69. Cleveland Rockwell
Harrison Lake, B.C.
Water colour, 1895
14 3/8 x 20 1/4

70. Cleveland Rockwell
Looking down the Inlet, near Juneau
Water colour, 1884
13 3/4 x 19 7/8

gence immediately imparts a sense of depth to the picture. The mountains, like the foreground, are precisely and correctly painted, with each feature carefully defined. The definition itself is controlled, so that the mountains become fainter as they recede in the distance; by this means, the effect of atmospheric distortion is created. This strong emphasis on realism typifies Rockwell's paintings, and stands in sharp contrast to the work of painters like Hammond and Bell-Smith.

George Horne Russell travelled in the Rockies in the early part of the twentieth century, painting on commission. Russell was born in 1861 in Banff, Scotland, and studied at the Aberdeen Art School and at the South Kensington Art School in London under Alphonse Legros and Sir George Reid. He came to Montreal in 1890, and continued to live there except for the summers which he spent in St. Andrews, New Brunswick. Russell was appointed an associate of the Royal Canadian Academy in 1909, and a full member in 1918; he served as president from 1922 to 1926.

The two Russell paintings in this book indicate the increasing tendency towards large-format work. Each was commissioned by a different railroad. "Roche Miette, Jasper National Park" (Illustration No. 72) was painted for the Canadian National Railway, and hung in their board room for a number of years. The scale of the painting is monumental. The camp and the figure in the canoe are totally overshadowed to the point of insignificance by the grandeur of the mountain rising immediately from the water. Russell has greatly exaggerated the scale in order to emphasize the immensity that can be seen and felt in the mountain. There is some detail in the foreground, but the principal focus is the massive mountain. The entire composition is dominated by it - Russell is not concerned with creating continuous space, as was Rockwell, for instance. Instead the mountain fills up the total canvas with an overwhelming power.

"Kicking Horse Pass" (Illustration No. 71) has this effect, of a landscape that totally dominates any human activity. This painting was commissioned by the C.P.R., and for a number of years hung in the Palliser Hotel in Calgary. Instead of looking up at the landscape in this painting, Russell has the viewer looking down. The train with its lighted coaches becomes merely a superficial intrusion. Russell uses loose brushstrokes to give maximum emphasis to the rocks, water, and trees. He is not interested in realistically defining each characteristic, but vividly illustrates the mas-

71. George H. Russell
Kicking Horse Pass
Oil, 1900
77 3/4 x 59 1/4

72. George H. Russell
Roche Miette, Jasper National Park
Oil, no date
71 7/8 x 48 1/4

73. Leonard M. Davis
Mountain Landscape, Bow Valley
Oil, 1918
36 x 54

sive overlapping of basic elements. Once again Russell seems to lock in the space of the landscape - he does not attempt to provide a continuous panorama of space.

Leonard M. Davis was an American who travelled to both western Canada and Alaska. He was born in Winchendon, Massachusetts, in 1864, and received his formal art training at the Art Students' League, New York, and the Académie Julien, Paris.

Davis was the first painter to be a guest at the E.P. Ranch in Alberta, which was owned by the Prince of Wales. Davis made a number of paintings of the ranch, four of which were purchased by the Prince of Wales, and twenty-three by the Canadian Government. Davis visited Calgary in 1917 or 1918 on his return from a trip to Alaska. Through the efforts of the Alpine Club, an exhibition was held at the public library, which was well received. While in Calgary Davis was a guest of Mr. D. G. Campbell, and as payment for the hospitality, offered to donate several paintings. However, the provision was that Campbell was to pay for the frames and for their transportation from New York. In order to cover this expense, Campbell sold "stock" at $25.00 per share, with the painting then going to the Chamber of Commerce. This proved to be quite successful, and in fact one person offered to pay $50.00 if Davis would include some cattle. This he did not do.

"Mountain Landscape, Bow Valley" (Illustration No. 73) and "Harvesting, Nobleford" (Illustration No. 55) were two paintings that were part of this agreement. Both paintings are relatively large, measuring three feet by four and a half feet.

"Harvesting, Nobleford" vividly illustrates early autumn on the prairies. The flat countryside extends horizontally to an undefined depth, articulated by stooks of wheat. The sky gracefully covers the entire landscape. Davis uses the rich and subtly varied colours of the prairies to emphasize the light and provide a complex mosaic. The textured quality of the paint most effectively conveys a tactile sense of the freshly cut crops. It is a painting that not only presents the visual images but also the *feeling* of the prairies.

"Mountain Landscape, Bow Valley" has a similarly rich, textured quality. The quiet, almost idyllic setting seems as if it had never before been observed or visited. The detailing of the foliage beside the calm blue water is set against a soft undulating mountain. The other mountains gradually recede to the left, conveying a definite sense of depth and atmosphere.

The artists who visited the West after the coming of the railway were professional both in training and in their ability to popularize their work. Their participation in societies, publications, and exhibitions brought an artistic exposure of the western environment far beyond anything the pre-1880's artists could achieve. This popularization was the key contribution of the late nineteenth-century artists in western Canada.

At about the time Russell and Davis were painting "Kicking Horse Pass, Jasper National Park" and "Mountain Landscape, Bow Valley", the first resident artists were already beginning to settle in western Canada. From 1900 onwards several non-professional artists were living and painting in the area, although it was not for another twenty or thirty years that established professional artists took up residence in the West in significant numbers. As their ranks increased, however, an important change began to take place in the visual record being compiled of western Canada. For the first time, an interpretation of the land was coming from the hands of the artists who lived and worked in the environment.

3. The First Residents

Overleaf:
74. H. Eric Bergman
Strange Rock Formations
Wood engraving, no date
6 1/8 x 8 1/8

75. Sara Mary Blake
Falls on the Middle Fork
of Old Man's River
Water colour, 1889
9 1/4 x 18 7/8

With the completion of the Canadian Pacific Railway, a tremendous influx of settlers began moving to the new land that was being opened up. Included in their ranks were numerous professional artists. Although many artists had travelled west prior to this, it was not until the turn of the century that they began to take up residence in western Canada in substantial numbers.

By the 1920's an ever widening circle of very gifted resident artists were painting in various parts of the West. Art schools and art societies appeared in several western cities. A new cultural climate was developing, which was to explore the full range of western Canadian imagery. These artists brought with them a trained eye and a thorough knowledge of technique. Many of them were trained in Europe, others in eastern Canada and the United States. While some continued to show a distinct European quality in their work throughout their careers, others adjusted their approach to the more massive, colourful environment of western Canada.

Perhaps the most significant attribute of these first resident artists was their desire and ambition to explore, record, and re-record the landscape. The result of their work was a completely new body of art, a new expression of the continually changing spectrum of colour, space, and forms that is so characteristic of this part of the world.

One of the earliest of the resident artists was Sara Mary Blake, a gifted amateur who lived in Alberta before the turn of the century. Sara Blake was born in 1864 in Galway, Ireland, where she spent her early years. She attended a convent at St. Leonards-on-the-Sea in Sussex, taking art courses among her general studies. After she finished school, she lived in England and France with her mother and two sisters. In 1887 she travelled to Canada to join her brother Frank, who had started a ranch on the north fork of the Old Man River in Alberta. In 1890 she married Alfred Lynch-Staunton, who had come west in 1877 with a detachment of the North West Mounted Police.

"Falls on the Middle Fork of Old Man's River" (Illustration No. 75) was painted in 1889, shortly after Blake arrived in Canada. The basic quality of this water colour is its simple, straightforward, honest representation. Details such as the spindly trees and the rocks in the river are deliberately presented; the artist does not exaggerate any of the compositional components, but paints them purely as they appear. The result is a refreshing and simplified look at the landscape that has a character and charm all its own.

John D. Curren was born in Scotland in 1852,

76. J.D. Curren
Sinclair Canyon
Oil, no date
16 1/4 x 12

77. J. D. Curren
Johnson's Canyon
Oil, no date
16 1/4 x 12

78. J. D. Curren
Mt. Rundle, Banff
Oil, no date
12 x 16 1/4

and came to Alberta in 1886, settling in Cochrane. Prior to his death in Banff in 1940, he had been among other things a prospector, a miner, and a photographer.

Curren, like Sara Mary Blake, had virtually no training as an artist. His paintings are not sophisticated, but instead demonstrate strong qualities of honesty and strength. Simple, precise forms, often slightly exaggerated, emphasize the various landscape elements. There is a great vividness to the works; in the best sense, they are primitive art.

For example, in "Sinclair Canyon" (Illustration No. 76), Curren brings a massive vertical cliff out to the picture plane on the right that partially fills the vertical frame. The cliff, having little definition and being dominated by its placement in the composition, presents only a paper-thin image without a high degree of three dimensionality. The left side of the painting opens up to show the depth of the canyon. The water is almost glass-like, with rocks that seem to rest upon its surface or jut out abruptly. The rocks, like the cliff, seem to be a "construction", in that there is an implication of monumentality. Nevertheless, the two-dimensional image persists.

Another canyon scene, "Johnson's Canyon" (Illustration No. 77), has some of the same characteristics. By increasing the sense of shadow along the ridge, however, Curren creates a stronger sense of mass. The trees resemble verticle poles with small dabs of paint applied to them. As in "Sinclair Canyon", the painting is a very simplified composition, uncluttered by numerous detailed landscape elements.

"Winter Scene" (Illustration No. 81) is basically the same centralized composition as the previous two paintings, using trees to flank the centre which in turn recedes towards Mt. Rundle. As in the other paintings, the trees are built up with small dabs of white paint: they are quite large in the foreground, and then diminish very sharply in a pronounced and over-exaggerated perspective. The snow rests gently on the surface and periphery of the pool, yet at the same time seems detached from the water. Rising out of the background is Mt. Rundle, which Curren vividly expresses as an outline with very little surface articulation. This same characteristic is evident in the sky, snow, and water, where only minimal detail is shown beyond the basic outline.

"Mt. Rundle, Banff" (Illustration No. 78) is a panoramic view. The tree on the left establishes a high ground, from which the painting descends

Top Left:
79. J.D. Curren
C.P.R. Tracks
Oil, no date
10 7/8 x 11 1/8

Bottom Left:
80. J.D. Curren
The Barrier on the Kananaskis River
Oil, no date
9 7/8 x 11 1/4

81. J.D. Curren
Winter Scene
Oil, no date
11 3/4 x 10 1/4

sharply. The zig-zig of the water carries the eye into the composition, and then the curve of the mountains in the middleground gently frames Mt. Rundle. The articulation and simplicity of composition are strongly evident in the painting. Minimal brushstrokes in broad areas form the rocks, water, trees, and mountains, without emphasizing any detail. The honesty with which Curren portrays the landscape without romanticizing what he sees gives a freshness and charm that are exceptionally appealing.

Both Blake and Curren are examples of the talented amateur who painted the West. In general their work is marked by several characteristic features, such as the technique of using basic colours and relationships of form to achieve an abstracted effect, and by their relative simplicity of interpretation.

John Innes spent most of his life in the West painting and recording historical events. He did not turn to serious painting, however, until the turn of the century.

Innes was born in London, Ontario, in 1864, and was educated at Hellmouth College, London; King's College, Sherbourne, England; and Dufferin Military Academy. During his schooling Innes took some art instruction, which obviously affected the course of his future life: "As the years passed it became increasingly evident that unkind fate had palmed off an artist on my sorrowing family.... Therefore it was determined to send me to college in the old country - no doubt in the hope that I might reform. In England I became rapidly worse."[1]

Upon returning from England, Innes decided to travel west in 1883. He came to Calgary, where he set up a corral and stable for a short time before establishing a ranch at the mouth of the High River. During this period he drew a number of cartoons for the Calgary *Herald* including one that sent the publisher to jail for contempt of court.

After leaving his ranch he settled in Banff, and for a brief time published a newspaper called *Mountain Echoes*. He also worked for the federal government in developing Banff National Park, but was dismissed from that job, according to an official, for making statements "not considered to be in the public interest." In 1892 he left Alberta for Vancouver, where he and A.M.R. Gordon published the short-lived newspaper *The Hornet*.

In 1895 Innes left for the East and worked for the Toronto *Mail and Empire* as an illustrator and writer. Between then and 1913 he participated in the South African War as an illustrator, worked for the Hearst organization in New York, and drew freelance weekly cartoons for numerous United States newspapers.

In 1913 Innes returned to Canada, settling in Vancouver, where he lived until his death in 1941. One of the reasons for his return was that he had developed an idea to paint an historical series related to the Canadian West. In 1915 he exhibited sixteen canvases with the title "Chunks of the Western Epic". The series was interrupted during World War I, as Innes was obliged once again to turn to newspaper illustration in order to make a living.

After the war Innes found a patron, Arthur P. Denby, who enabled him to complete two illustrated series on western Canadian history. More paintings were added to "Chunks of the Western Epic" to complete the "Epic of Western Canada" collection. The second series was the "Epic of Transportation" series, or "From Trail to Rail", which comprised twenty-one large canvases.

One of the paintings from the second series was "Battle of the Rocks" (Illustration No. 82). This painting provides a most unusual perspective of the mountains by having the viewer look down through a bank of clouds to a valley far below. There is almost the sensation of observing from the vantage point of an airplane. The result is an immense exaggerated landscape, with a scale so monumental that the train near the floor of the mountain becomes totally insignificant to the painting. Scale and perspective are Innes's primary interests. He does not attempt to include detail, but instead uses broad brushstrokes to build up the fortress-like mountains. By sheer size he conveys the romanticized concept of the Rockies. Like Russell and Davis, Innes overpowers the viewer through his dynamic representation and the immense format.

A painter who took up residence in British Columbia in the early twentieth century was Thomas W. Fripp. Born in London, England, in 1864, Fripp studied under his father, George Arthur Fripp, an established English water-colour painter. Fripp also studied at St. John's Wood Art School and the Royal Academy Art School from 1887 to 1890. After a visit to Italy, Fripp came to Canada in 1893 and settled on a ranch in British Columbia. As the result of an injury, he had to give up farming, and subsequently turned to painting as a means of livelihood. He continued to paint the mountains and the Pacific Coast until his death in 1931. He was a founder and the

Opposite:
82. John Innes
Battle of the Rocks
Oil, no date
50 1/4 x 42

first President of the British Columbia Society of Artists.

Fripp only occasionally worked in oil, concentrating instead on water colour. The painting "Mt. Fairview from Mt. Temple" (Illustration No. 104) vividly illustrates his rich use of colour and a delicacy in building up forms. The rocks in the foreground have a solidity obtained by subtle gradations in tone and the use of light. The misty white of the snow and clouds gradually moves the eye to the gently outlined mountain in the background. Fripp does not try to show a total panoramic scene, but concentrates on one aspect of the mountain environment.

Fripp's paintings are very different from those of Innes, his contemporary in British Columbia. While Innes was basically interested in a historical portrayal and was very powerful in his images, Fripp had a delicacy and a greater interest in an aesthetic appreciation of the landscape. In his sensitivity to the nuances of the painting, Fripp was closer in his approach to two other British Columbia artists, Charles H. Scott and Ina D.D. Uhthoff, in treating the landscape in an artistic fashion. On the other hand, both Scott and Uhthoff showed more of the massive energy of the land. On balance, Fripp was more closely identifiable with an English understanding of the landscape, while Scott and Uhthoff attempted to take on a more Canadian style in the manner of the Group of Seven.

Charles H. Scott was born in Glasgow, Scotland, in 1886. He studied art at the Glasgow School of Art, and then travelled and pursued additional studies throughout Belgium, Germany, France, and Italy. He came to Calgary in 1912 to be Art Supervisor of Public Schools, and stayed until 1914, when he returned to Scotland. He came back to Canada in 1919, this time assuming a similar post in Vancouver, where he remained until his death in 1964. For twenty-seven years, from 1925 to 1952, Scott was head of the Vancouver School of Art. During his tenure there he developed an influential and energetic program, bringing both F.H. Varley and J.W.G. Macdonald, among others, to the school. Scott himself was profoundly influenced by his contact with these two Group of Seven painters, in particular Varley.

In the seascape "A West Coast Rain" (Illustration No. 84), a tremendous sensation of space is created. The curving rocks in the immediate foreground establish the picture plane from which the landscape then recedes. Broad horizontal bands give a textural quality to the beach and water,

83. Charles H. Scott
The Winding River Fraser
Oil, no date
11 x 15 1/8

84. Charles H. Scott
A West Coast Rain
Oil, no date
12 x 15

85. Charles H. Scott
The Mighty Fraser
Oil, no date
11 7/8 x 15

86. Charles H. Scott
Mountains and Lake Garibaldi
Oil, no date
12 x 14 1/2

and also create a sense of perspective. A faint but obvious line marks the horizon. The sky is painted with wide, short brushstrokes that reinforce the mood already suggested by the other elements. The feeling of the low rain clouds is vividly implied.

Another landscape by Scott, "The Winding River Fraser" (Illustration No. 83), has the same strong brushstrokes and thick use of paint as "A West Coast Rain". Scott suggests the strength of the mountains and sky with a heavy application of the brush and very little articulation of detail. Clouds are also created by wide brushstrokes, some straight, some spiral, and some curved. The randomness of the clouds contrasts with the concentrated massiveness of the mountains.

"The Mighty Fraser" (Illustration No. 85) is similar to "The Winding River Fraser". The feeling of depth is emphasized by the twisting of the river as it moves towards the centre of the painting, and by the overlapping of the mountains on the right. The texture of the paint builds up the gently curved mountains into massive units juxtaposed together. Scott captures the *essence* of the mountains. "The Mighty Fraser" and "The Winding River Fraser" both convey power and monumenality without limiting the imagination through a photographically specific image.

Ina D. D. Uhthoff was born in Glasgow in 1889, and like Charles Scott attended the Glasgow School of Art. She taught high school for a few years before coming to Victoria in 1926. There she opened a teaching studio, which built up through the years into a wide range of classes. For two years, 1929 and 1930, Uhthoff and Emily Carr sponsored classes that were given by Mark Tobey. Uhthoff's own classes were very successful, and were in fact the genesis of the Victoria School of Art, which was formed under the auspices of the Provincial Department of Education. She continued to teach in Victoria for a number of years, and was also involved in the formation of the Art Gallery of Greater Victoria. In addition to these activities, she also wrote an art column for the *Daily Colonist*. She died in Ontario in 1971.

Two paintings by Uhthoff, "Castle Mountain"

87. I.D.D. Uhthoff
Glacier and Moraine
Oil, 1934
23 7/8 x 36

102

88. I.D.D. Uhthoff
Castle Mountain
Oil, 1943
12 x 14

(Illustration No. 88) and "Glacier and Moraine" (Illustration No. 87), effectively illustrate the massiveness of the land. In "Castle Mountain" (since re-named Mt. Eisenhower), broad, sweeping brushstrokes pull the foot of the mountain up to the vertical rocks on the left, and curved areas of paint build up the hills on the right. Shorter wider brushstrokes emphasize the sculptural, cubic quality of the mountain top. The mountain has an immense *presence* as it rises practically to fill the format. The dominance is further emphasized by the minimal treatment of the sky. "Glacier and Moraine" has a similar massive and dynamic quality. The plastic glacier winds, almost lazily, between the rocks positioned close to the picture plane. The starkness is intensified by the lone dead tree on the left of the painting.

In both paintings, Uhthoff vividly conveys the power of the western countryside. Like Scott she minimizes the landscape's elements and emphasizes its basic structure and form. It is this simplicity that makes both their work so powerful.

In the early twentieth century a number of genuinely outstanding artists emigrated to Canada and settled in the West. This development provided a tremendous impetus to the artistic and cultural life of western Canada. One such man who would profoundly affect western Canadian art and gain an international reputation was Walter J. Phillips.

The son of an itinerant Methodist minister, Phillips was born in 1884 at Barton-on-Humber, Lincolnshire. He attended Bourne College, Quinton, Birmingham, where he excelled in drawing and also won a general proficiency prize of £20. The money assisted him in travelling to South Africa, where he stayed from 1903 to 1908. During the five years he spent there, Phillips worked as a newspaper reporter, diamond digger, lawyer's clerk, and peripatetic trader.

Upon his return to England, Phillips tried to make his living as a commercial artist and then as a freelance artist. The latter undertaking did not prove successful, so he became art master at Bishop Woodsworth School in Salisbury. During his time there, Phillips developed his watercolour technique, and had his first one-man exhibition in 1911, at Salisbury. In 1912 he exhibited at the Royal Academy.

In the summer of 1913 Phillips and his wife emigrated to Canada, settling in Winnipeg, Manitoba. He was appointed art instructor at St. John's Technical High School, where he remained until 1924, when he and his family returned to England to live. Their time in England lasted only ten months; Phillips returned to live permanently in Canada until his death in 1963.

Shortly after his arrival in Winnipeg, Phillips met and formed a friendship with Cyril Barraud. While Phillips had concentrated primarily on water colours and excelled at this medium, through Barraud he learned the art of etching. When Barraud went overseas during World War I, Phillips bought his tools and press. Although he was intrigued with this medium and proved to be very adept at it, he felt the limitations of the absence of colour. This led him to his first attempts with colour woodcut prints, a medium that was to gain him international acclaim. Between 1917, the time of his first experiments, and 1952, Phillips created and produced about 160 different woodblocks.

During the ten months he spent in England, Phillips had the opportunity to meet and exchange ideas with numerous colour print makers, including William Gyles, Sydney Lee, Allen W. Seaby, and Y. Urushibara. Urushibara taught Phillips a Japanese method of sizing paper.

After his return to Winnipeg in 1925, Phillips's career as a creative artist developed impressively. During the next few years he produced his greatest number of woodcut prints, although he continued with them at a slower pace over a considerable period of time.

Also upon his return to Winnipeg Phillips joined the staff of the Winnipeg *Tribune* newspaper, writing a weekly column "Art and Artists", which he continued until 1942. The year 1926 saw the publication of his book *The Technique of the Colour Woodcut*. Phillips was an extremely good writer, and his articles on art contain an insight and perception that is still valid today.

In 1940 Phillips joined the staff of the Banff Summer School of Fine Arts, and was to return for a number of summers to teach and do his own work. He moved to Calgary in 1941 and taught at the Southern Alberta Institute of Technology and Art for a short period of time. Following a move to Banff, Phillips settled in Victoria where he lived until his death.

Phillips concentrated almost exclusively on western Canadian subjects for his water colours and prints. Lake of the Woods was Phillips's primary source for water colours from 1914 to 1924. From 1925 to 1935 the prairies provided his main themes, while from 1936 he concentrated mainly on the Rocky Mountains. The West Coast also was a source for subject matter from 1926 on.

89. Walter J. Phillips
Landscape
Water colour, no date
7 1/4 x 9

90. Walter J. Phillips
Lake Kalamalka
Water colour, 1947
6 1/4 x 8 3/4

91. Walter J. Phillips
Vapours Round the Mountain Curled
Colour woodcut, no date
16 x 18

92. Walter J. Phillips
Landscape
Water colour, 1945
5 1/2 x 9 1/2

93. Walter J. Phillips
Landscape
Water colour, 1949
6 1/2 x 10 3/4

94. Walter J. Phillips
Landscape
Water colour, 1949
6 1/2 x 9 3/4

95. Walter J. Phillips
Landscape
Water colour, 1946
9 1/2 x 11

96. Walter J. Phillips
Wenkchemna Pass
Water colour, 1948
7 x 9 1/2

97. Walter J. Phillips
Waterfall
Water colour, no date
5 x 9

98. Walter J. Phillips
Saskatchewan Glacier
Water colour, 1950
4 3/4 x 9

99. Walter J. Phillips
Landscape
Water colour, 1946
7 1/4 x 9 3/4

100. Walter J. Phillips
Landscape
Water colour, 1946
7 1/4 x 9 3/4

101. Walter J. Phillips
Peachland, Lake Okanagan
Water colour, 1946
4 3/4 x 9 3/4

102. Walter J. Phillips
Assiniboine and Quartz Mountains
Water colour, 1949
5 3/4 x 10 3/4

103. Walter J. Phillips
Blue Douglas Fir, Banff
Water colour, 1952
15 7/8 x 18

104. Thomas W. Fripp
Mt. Fairview from Mt. Temple
Water colour, 1918
10 3/4 x 14

105. Walter J. Phillips
Rundle through a Screen of Poplars
Water colour, 1952
14 1/2 x 21 1/2

106. Walter J. Phillips
Lake of the Woods
Water colour, no date
7 1/4 x 9

Phillips's water colours are exquisite, magnificent portrayals of the western environment. Duncan Campbell Scott wrote of Phillips in his monograph on the artist published in 1947:

A Phillips water colour has . . . a wide appeal. First there is always a well-thought-out design, often unusual and at all times satisfying. Invariably it is based on nature, but with selection and control of figure or landscape features to achieve the desired end. Phillips never feels it necessary to distort (or resort to distortion). He finds in nature truthfully recorded all the beauty of form and line needed. These latter are things especially to look for and enjoy in his work: the drawing of trees in detail or mass, the rhythmic lines of the countryside, the formation of mountain architecture, of the exciting movement of rushing water, all delineated with special emphasis on the decorative patterns wherever in nature.

Phillips has a fine feeling for colour. Each picture has its own scheme for colour, with pervading hue, its harmonies and contrasts. And lastly there is the masterly handling of the medium. A Phillips sky with its atmospheric depths and tender gradations is the last word in water-colour manipulation. Anyone who has attempted the medium will also appreciate the way in which washes are applied throughout the picture with the bloom of the paint undisturbed by rubbing or re-working, and the skill with which sparkling whites are left where required. In all this technical virtuosity Phillips is unexcelled on this continent . . . . [2]

"Blue Douglas Fir, Banff" (Illustration No. 103) and "Rundle through a Screen of Poplars" (Illustration No. 105) are two examples of Phillips's finished water colours. Both paintings are carefully thought out and extremely well balanced. Generally, the compositions have a pronounced foreground, a minor middleground, and a strong background. Phillips meticulously balanced all the elements to pull the painting together to form a total unit.

In "Blue Douglas Fir, Banff" a tree standing close to the picture plane rises from the rocky textured foreground to establish a sense of space in the painting. Only the faintly suggested trees

107. Walter J. Phillips
Landscape
Water colour, no date
7 1/2 x 10 1/2

108. Walter J. Phillips
Howe Sound
Colour woodcut, 1935
10 1/4 x 12 1/4

in the green band in the middleground form a transition to the jagged mountains behind.

"Rundle through a Screen of Poplars" is an equally careful rendering, with the same emphasis on the fore, middle, and backgrounds. On the left of the painting, Phillips subtly presents a number of tall, thin, soft-looking trees positioned fairly close to the front. To balance the foreground is Mt. Rundle in the background at the right, massive and dominating as it sweeps towards the trees. The composition strongly pulls the viewer into the painting and provides a positive-negative relationship of textures and shapes.

Phillips does not provide a high degree of detailed realism in his work, but he unquestionably does paint clear, recognizable forms. His colours are rich and crisp in their outline, and give an essentially three-dimensional quality to the landscapes. There is never a mistake or the accidental creation of a form; every component is sure, perfectly placed, and strongly defined.

Phillips's sketchbooks illustrate just how wide-ranging was the study he made of the landscape, both for his water colours and his colour woodcuts. The sketches not only provide the opportunity to look at the total landscape, but also to examine in detail each of the component parts. Phillips often worked out a number of versions with continual refinements and changes before satisfying himself that the artistic concept had sufficient merit to warrant completion of the finished work. The sketchbooks provide a rare insight into Phillips's techniques.

The sketches range from wide panoramic views to small intimate studies of specific features such as a waterfall. The spontaneity evident in the sketches gives them startling freshness, and distinguishes them sharply from the finished water colour. The deliberate use of technique and the careful construction and composition seen in the finished water colour and also in the woodcuts are less evident in the sketches. Undoubtedly the rapidity in doing the sketches resulted in this effect.

Some of the sketches are briefly outlined with pencil, but only to the extent of defining forms, rather than representing every detail. In other sketches he worked directly with the brush. The sketches are small in scale, ranging from two by four inches to seven by ten inches. Despite the small size, the precision that is clearly the mark of a Phillips painting is unmistakable.

Certain typical qualities are common to most of the sketches. The rocks, usually in the fore-

109. Walter J. Phillips
Mountain Torrent
Colour woodcut, 1926
10 x 12

110. Walter J. Phillips
Leaf of Gold
Colour woodcut, 1941
9 1/4 x 12 3/4

ground, have a very pronounced three-dimensional quality, and a great sense of solidity. The treatment in water colour fills in the forms and adds texture and substance to them. On the other hand, water is "simplified" in comparison to the inter-relationship of colours and shapes of the rocks. Lakes usually are placed in the middleground and are formed from broad bands of colour. This suggests calmness, a contrast with the jagged rocks. Where the wind has caused movement of the water, the effect is created by short strokes laid on the broad colour.

The trees in the sketches usually resemble those in the water colour "Rundle through a Screen of Poplars". Phillips clearly expresses the shape of the trees but does not itemize every detail. Broad areas of yellow, green, brown, or red clearly suggest the branches and leaves.

The rolling hills usually positioned in the middleground are formed by gently curving lines counterbalanced by other forms that create almost a mirror image. Often the hills meet at a low point above which a mountain rises upward. The hills are a soft area between the more dynamic and busier back and foregrounds that create a transition to lead the eye into the painting.

The backgrounds vividly depict the multifaceted forms seen in the Rockies and the other western mountain ranges. The mountains tower majestically against a soft blue sky or clouds. Small precise areas of colour enunciate the forms and again convey a high degree of three-dimensionality.

The skies are treated very softly in the watercolour sketches. Broad bands of colour are used for the sky, with the white paper showing through to form the clouds. Instead of painting clouds themselves, Phillips often paints around the shape of the clouds. In some cases the clouds are built up into very plastic rubbery forms that almost seem suspended from the sky. As in the finished water colours, Phillips vividly catches the variety of colours in the landscape. He is not timid in his approach. Rich intense colour is very typical of his work.

The other medium that Phillips used and excelled at was colour woodcuts. Phillips wrote of this medium,

The art of print-making is a distinct responsibility. A poor painting may be a crime, but only one: a poor print is a crime multiplied by the size of the edition. But once the artist has come to terms with his conscience there is a certain amount of fun in the craft, especially when the medium is wood.

Wood must be humoured. It seems to be a sentient thing. It warps and twists, expands and contracts, it cracks and splits as if protesting its mutilation.[3]

In the woodcut medium, an artist carves in reverse on a block of wood. The image that remains after the wood has been removed is the part printed on the paper. For each colour it is necessary to have a separate woodblock. This greatly adds to the difficulty of the operation, as the carving on each block has to be exact to register with the other blocks. Phillips worked as many as seven blocks to get one print. The craftsmanship required had to be excellent, and with Phillips, it always was.

Four woodblock prints illustrate the high degree of technical ability and artistic sensitivity typical of Phillips's prints. Each print is an unusual composition. In "Mountain Torrent" (Illustration No. 109), instead of looking down at a waterfall, the viewer seems to be positioned in the stream itself and looking up at the falls. The high degree of texture and variety of forms create an interesting glimpse of one small area of the mountains.

In "Vapours Round the Mountain Curled" (Illustration No. 91), Phillips once again focuses on one aspect of the mountain landscape. An elegant design of clouds wraps itself around a partially hidden mountain peak. Very soft greys are used throughout the prints. The composition is highlighted by the intense red of the fireweed. The result is almost a mystical understanding of the landscape.

"Howe Sound" (Illustration No. 108), in contrast to the previous woodcuts, is a panoramic view. A huge expanse of water recedes gently into the background to meet a range of snowcapped mountains. As such, this is a traditional view, with a conventional immediate foreground, middleground, and background. What makes the composition unusual is the umbrella-like tree in the immediate foreground, that covers almost all of the space of the picture and yet at the same time reduces the sense of space by imposing limits on the sweepingness of the view.

"Leaf of Gold" (Illustration No. 110) in some respects accomplishes the same artistic objectives as "Howe Sound". A tree branch comes in from the immediate foreground on the left and curves across the picture plane. This establishes the initial visual contact, from which the landscape

111. H. Eric Bergman
Snow Scene
Wood engraving, no date
8 1/8 x 4 1/2

then recedes. As in "Howe Sound" the foliage serves primarily as an illusionary device to involve the viewer more totally in the landscape.

To conclude, Phillips had a unique ability to examine and then record the environment. Through his work a great awareness of the beauty of the landscape has resulted. No artist could achieve more.

H. Eric Bergman was born in Dresden, Germany, in 1893. After attending public school and three years of trade school there, he came to Canada in 1913, the same year as Phillips. He arrived in Toronto and a year later moved to Winnipeg, where he was to live until his death in 1958. In Winnipeg he worked as a wood engraver, retoucher, and photo engraver. In 1922 his employer, Fred Brigden, and Walter J. Phillips inspired Bergman to turn his talents to non-commercial art. During the next thirty-six years he gained a national and international reputation and exhibited in cities throughout the world. He worked in water colour, pencil, colour woodcuts, and silverpoint drawings. His forte was wood engraving, an exacting medium but one that can present dynamic and totally visually absorbing images.

Robert Ayre, a Canadian art critic, characterized Bergman: "he has a profound respect for wood and paper, ink and tools; he believes in being faithful to his medium, in exploring the wood but never violating its nature; he has no patience with slipshod work, it is not in him to be hit-and-miss, he has nothing but scorn for trickery; eye and hand are the trained and disciplined servants of his integrity. The result is that his subjects are chosen for appropriateness to the wood; his compositions are carefully built, but care does not thin out vitality, for they are lovingly built; his orchestration of texture is full of diversity, his range of colour wide, his whites and blacks can be dazzling, he can modulate from black to white through an astonishing variety of tones, each falling unerringly into its place in the scheme."[4]

Bergman very patiently and carefully developed each wood engraving. The precision evident in his work took a high degree of technical ability and emotional control. As he said himself, "a wood engraving cannot be hacked out in a wave of emotional excitement or as we sometimes say, in a fit of artistic temperament. Every time it must be well conceived and express a precise and definite emotional idea. The artist using this medium must have complete control over his emotions as well as over his tools and material."[5] Bergman

112. H. Eric Bergman
Burned-over Trees
Wood engraving, no date
5 3/8 x 7 3/8

113. H. Eric Bergman
Oaks and Wind
Wood engraving, 1934
5 5/8 x 7 1/8

114. H. Eric Bergman
Fir Trees in Snow
Wood engraving, 1926
4 3/8 x 4 1/8

115. H. Eric Bergman
Approaching Storm
Woodcut, 1927
7 3/8 x 10 1/8

would often spend his evenings listening to classical music, such as Beethoven, Wagner, and Stravinsky, while concentrating on a block of wood.

Bergman's main subject matter came from Northern Manitoba, Lake of the Woods, Eastern Ontario, and the Rocky Mountains. He concentrated both on total scenes as well as on small, intimate views of the landscape, such as flowers and leaves. He very seldom produced the wide panoramic views seen in Phillips's work.

Bergman used lines and dots, with variations, to build up subtle tonalities and express a three-dimensional quality. In "Oaks and Wind" (Illustration No. 113), close crosshatching of lines forms a gently waving foreground. The trees seem to rest on the ground and wind upwards in twisting, textural forms. There is little feeling that they are rooted in the soil. In contrast to the relatively heavy lines of the trees, the leaves are delicately outlined, giving a lush quality to the upper part of the print. In this particular composition, Bergman has brought most of the detail work to the foreground; beyond the trees the lighter lines gently lead the eye to the horizon.

"Burned-over Trees" (Illustration No. 112), another wood engraving print, illustrates the rich visual texture in the foreground and on the trees. Curving parallel lines follow the shape of the rocks to emphasize the depth of the scene. The trees are richly built up by small curved lines that are more closely spaced at the edge to give plasticity. Moss, formed by numerous dots, highlights and punctuates the texture of the trees. As in "Oaks and Wind", the major attention is given to the foreground, with very little articulation to

Below:
117. H. Eric Bergman
Trees
Wood engraving, 1924
4 13/16 x 4

Above:
116. H. Eric Bergman
Waterfall
Wood engraving, no date
6 x 4 1/4

Below:
118. H. Eric Bergman
Sunlight on Trees
Woodcut, 1924
10 x 7 3/4

Above:
119. H. Eric Bergman
Little Sand Lake, Minaki
Linocut, 1923
10 x 7 7/8

the background.

The richness of Bergman's treatment of trees is clearly evident in "Snow Scene" (Illustration No. 111) . Subtle scalloped lines form the bark, and thin interlocking twigs provide a delicate balance in the composition. By locating the tree close to the picture plane, a screen is provided through which the rest of the landscape is revealed. Bergman carefully has formed the soft snow to heighten the contrast behind the tree. The background becomes an outline of trees forming a definite separation from the tree in the foreground.

Bergman's colour woodcuts do not have the same high degree of detailing and visual texture as his wood engravings, nor, for that matter, the complexity and sophistication of Phillips's colour woodcuts. He used broad areas of colour, clearly outlined, to create the form such as the tree in "The Jackpine" (Illustration No. 121) and the rocks in "Approaching Storm" (Illustration No. 115). The colours in his woodcuts tend to be very subtle and are certainly less intense than the colours in W. J. Phillips's prints. The same compositional devices are used in the woodcuts as in the wood engravings, however. Bergman characteristically emphasized the trees in the foreground, and minimized the detailing in the background, giving only the shape of the landscape elements.

Phillips and Bergman had a tremendous impact on the pictorial representation of the West. Each had a deep respect for his medium, whether it was water-colour, pencil, woodcut, or wood engraving; an outstanding ability at his craft; and tremendous technical knowledge. Both artists set standards in printmaking that even today are seldom equalled.

One of the first artists to settle in Saskatchewan was a Scotsman, James Henderson. Born in Glasgow in 1871, he served a long apprenticeship as a lithographic artist, which enabled him to develop the technical skills necessary for his future work. While in Glasgow, Henderson also attended various art classes and galleries, a practice he continued when he moved to London.

Henderson emigrated to Winnipeg in 1909. After working there for a short time as a lithographic artist, he moved to Regina, where he did commercial art work and also secured a number of portrait commissions. In 1915 he and his wife moved to Fort Qu'Appelle, where they were to live until shortly before Henderson's death in 1951.

Arthur Hayworth, in his article "James Henderson of the Qu'Appelle Valley", must have echoed Henderson's own feelings for the area:

The Qu'Appelle Valley is about a mile in width and for the most part two hundred to three hundred feet in depth, and it extends from a point near Elbow on the South Saskatchewan River to the eastern boundary of the province, where the Qu'Appelle River joins the Assiniboine. The valley appears to have been in ancient times the bed of a mighty river which later changed its course. It has been cut out of the level plains by deep flowing water. In the course of centuries the sides of the valley have been changed by the flow of streams from the plains; hence the numerous coulees, beautifully wooded, and the rounded hills which, with the lakes, are features of the valley landscape. The south side of the valley is especially beautiful, with an abundance of poplars and ash, and many birches, elms and maples, as well as numerous varieties of shrubs and bushes. The whole area is a veritable paradise for the artist.[6]

This relatively circumscribed location in Saskatchewan was to become the source for nearly all of Henderson's paintings. He recorded every landscape element, every variation of light, colour, and form, every point of interest in the area. Only occasionally did he travel to other parts of Canada.

Henderson's life at Qu'Appelle was quiet. He did not actively sell or exhibit his paintings, and prospective buyers of his work were obliged to seek him out. One of the most significant events in his life came when the University of Saskatchewan conferred on him an honorary Doctor of Laws degree. Only two months later he died.

Henderson is well known both for his landscapes and his Indian paintings. He visited numerous Indian reserves and painted portraits of Cree, Saulteaux, Assiniboine, and Sioux. For these the latter tribe made him an honorary chief, giving him the name Wiciteowapi-Wicasa, meaning the man who paints the old men.

Henderson's landscapes have a vitality and presence to them. The composition is carefully built up to pull the viewer into the painting. Vertical units, usually trees, frame each side; then, by the shape of the valley or the river, a zigzag line leads the eye to the horizon. This is not a forced composition, but one that conveys the serenity of the land. The feeling of the big prairie sky is clearly expressed in these paintings, even though the vista is limited.

120. A.F. Kenderdine
The Road in the Valley
Oil, circa 1935
23 7/8 x 38 3/8

Henderson does not tightly limit the compositional components of the painting. Broad brushstrokes give shape to the individual trees as well as to the groups of trees, thereby providing the essence and colour of *trees*. The same is true of the way he paints streams, which become bands of colour rather than detailed portrayals. Snow is depicted by successive layers of paint that create a feeling of "snowiness", rather than carefully constructed snow drifts.

Henderson's colours are simultaneously rich and subtle, thereby reflecting the wide range of colouration found on the prairies themselves. In "Qu'Appelle Valley I" (Illustration No. 123), the snow becomes yellow and blue, providing highlights and shadows and creating a colourful mosaic. The same effect can be seen in "Qu'Appelle Valley II" (Illustration No. 124) in which one side of the valley is highlighted by yellow light while the other side is in shadowy blue. The rich and varied tones of the sky provide a soft balance to the various forms and colours of the land.

Augustus F. L. Kenderdine, who also settled in Saskatchewan, was a guiding force in the development of the various art schools in that province, as well as an important contributor in his own right to the art of western Canada. Kenderdine was born in Manchester, England. Although he disliked school, he showed an early talent for drawing, and consequently his godfather, Chevalier Lafosse, a Belgian artist, arranged for him to attend the Manchester School of Art. In 1884 Kenderdine was apprenticed to a fine art dealer, where he came into contact with numerous artists. This experience broadened his understanding of the subject.

Kenderdine left for France in 1891, where he worked as a bar keeper, among other jobs, while attending the Académie Julien in Paris. Upon returning he opened an art shop which was quite successful. During this period Kenderdine painted commissioned portraits and landscapes, for which he gained increasing recognition.

In 1908, tired of the art shop and partly influ-

121. H. Eric Bergman
The Jackpine
Woodcut, no date
8 1/4 x 9

122. H. Eric Bergman
Trees by Water
Woodcut, no date
10 3/4 x 9 1/2

123. James Henderson
Qu' Appelle Valley I
Oil, 1940
9 x 11 7/8

124. James Henderson
Qu'Appelle Valley II
Oil, no date
7 x 10

132

125. A.F. Kenderdine
Trees and Lake
Charcoal and water-colour wash, no date
14 1/2 x 19 1/2

126. A.F. Kenderdine
The Valley in Winter
Oil, circa 1935
17 x 21

127. A.F. Kenderdine
Windswept
Oil, circa 1920
26 1/2 x 34 1/4

128. A.F. Kenderdine
Autumn on the North Saskatchewan
Oil, no date
25 x 50

129. A.F. Kenderdine
Sutherland Trail
Oil, circa 1920-36
12 x 18 1/8

130. A. F. Kenderdine
Near Beaver Creek
Oil, circa 1920-36
8 7/8 x 12

131. A. F. Kenderdine
Emma Lake Spruce
Oil, circa 1930-47
11 1/2 x 8 1/2

enced by the story of the Barr Colonists, a group of English settlers who pioneered in the Lloydminster area in 1903, Kenderdine and his family emigrated to Canada. They homesteaded at Lashburn, Saskatchewan, and for the next few years concentrated on farming and ranching. He grew to love the country around the North Saskatchewan River, and gradually returned to painting as his primary occupation.

In 1920 Kenderdine was invited to set up a studio on the Saskatoon Campus of the University of Saskatchewan. This he did in the physics building, and within a short time was giving lessons to students. From this modest beginning grew the University Art Department.

During the 1920's, Kenderdine spent his winters teaching and his summers on field trips, mainly to the Rocky Mountains and the West Coast. In 1921 he did some paintings for the Canadian Pacific Railway. However, with the opening of Prince Albert National Park in 1927, Kenderdine discovered the beauty of the woods and lakes of northern Saskatchewan, and he began to spend his summers at Emma Lake.

In the early 1930's Kenderdine built a cottage at Emma Lake and also began to lay plans for a summer art school there. Although he tried to convince the University to finance the establishment of such a school, they were not interested. Finally in 1936, largely through the help of local people, he raised the first building of the new Emma Lake School on Murray Point. Eventually the University did agree to take over the Emma Lake School, due to its unquestionable success. Kenderdine taught there every summer until his death in 1947. The school has continued its growth to the present day, and has had a significant influence on western Canadian art.

Also in 1936 Kenderdine was transferred to the Regina campus of the University to build up the Art Department there. He was soon appointed a Professor of Art, and taught well past normal retirement age.

Kenderdine worked in both oils and charcoal. As might be expected, there is a freshness and spontaneity to his drawings, while the oil paintings have a structure and a more deliberate quality to them.

The charcoal drawings were done very quickly. The ground is built up by numerous solid areas of black that graduate through a series of tonal changes to white. There is very little definition to the landscape except for the trees. These are created by sure strokes of charcoal which form

132. A.F. Kenderdine
A Bit of Prairie
Charcoal, no date
19 x 24 3/4

133. A.F. Kenderdine
Emma Lake
Charcoal, no date
19 x 24 1/2

134. A. F. Kenderdine
Cutting the Road into Murray Point
Oil, circa 1935
12 x 9 1/8

135. A. F. Kenderdine
On the Front, Murray Point
Oil, no date
10 x 14

the trunks and branches. The trees tend to be almost two-dimensional forms creating a design, rather than an intrinsic part of the environment.

Kenderdine did not fill in the whole sheet of paper in his charcoals. This unfinished quality implies that only a momentary glimpse of the landscape was obtained by the artist. The oil paintings, on the other hand, are total, finished scenes, and are quite dissimilar to his charcoal work.

While Kenderdine relied mainly on tonal variations to separate the different landscape elements, he did occasionally add a small bit of colour for emphasis. For instance, in "Trees and Lake" (Illustration No. 125), he added small areas of yellow and green in the trees to the left, and a deep rich blue to the bushes between the two trees. The colour is often so subtle it is missed on the first glance. In the charcoal drawings, Kenderdine sometimes utilized a touch of water colour to add extra depth. This technique can be seen in the formation of the clouds in "Trees and Lake".

Kenderdine's oil paintings vividly illustrate the immensity of the prairie landscape. The land with its gently rolling hills recedes on a relatively flat plane, with the sky covering the entire vista. In "Sutherland Trail" (Illustration No. 129), the flatness of the land is emphasized by the winding road in the middle of the composition. The perspective is reinforced by the telephone poles on one side of the road and the fence posts on the other side. The starkly cloudless sky provides a contrast to the great variety of landscape features, thereby augmenting the sensation of vast space.

The same special emphasis can be seen in "The Valley in Winter" (Illustration No. 126) and "The Road in the Valley" (Illustration No. 120). In the latter the foliage near the foreground contrasts with the vividly expressed openness of the smooth hills and the sky. "The Valley in Winter" has much the same characteristics. The trees are placed close to the picture plane, with the hills located in such positions that they lead the eye into the painting. The representation of the trees is very simplified, with only a few brushstrokes forming the trunk and the branches, in much the same way as in the charcoal drawings.

Kenderdine usually tried to convey in his paintings a sense of the environment. In "Windswept" (Illustration No. 127), a painting of the foothills, the leaves and branches of the trees are pushed strongly to the right to convey a sense of wind. The cool colours intensify this effect. "Reflections" (Illustration No. 138) presents another mood. The rich colours of the sunset reflect across the surface of Emma Lake, providing similar, but not mirror, images. The sunset colours are located in a random fashion, but the partial symmetry of the composition gives a peaceful quality to the setting. A third mood, again different from the others, can be seen in "Autumn on the North Saskatchewan" (Illustration No. 128). The brown and orange colours of the foliage and the brown areas of greyness of the sky vividly present a feeling of the imminence of winter.

In many of his paintings like "Reflections" and "The Marsh, Emma Lake" (Illustration No. 139), Kenderdine used thick paint on the canvas to focus attention on the surface of the painting, although he only occasionally built up the forms themselves with paint; by this means, he most effectively suggests the rough sensuousness of the land. The result is an effect that complements the spatial quality of the painting.

Henderson and Kenderdine are probably the the two most significant painters in Saskatchewan during the first half of this century. Both artists were fascinated with the country, although each painted with a different understanding. Henderson, with his rich colour and intrinsic energy, tended to assume an identifiably Canadian attitude toward the land, while Kenderdine retained a European quality in his painting despite his vivid expressions of the environment. Nevertheless, each artist had a tremendous impact on the cultural life of Saskatchewan.

Alberta, like Saskatchewan and Manitoba, had a number of artists who emigrated to the province in the early twentieth century and made a significant contribution to the cultural life of the community. One such person was Alfred C. Leighton. Leighton was born in 1901 in Hastings, Sussex, England. After attending Hastings Grammar School, his father had him train as an architect. This only lasted for a short period of time, however, as Leighton was more interested in painting. His father finally agreed to allow him to attend the Brassey Institute of the Hastings Municipal School of Art, where he remained for two years. After a brief military career, during which he suffered injuries from an airplane accident that were to plague him for the rest of his life, Leighton had a short career as a toy designer, and then established a studio to make architectural models.

This proved to be a turning point in his career. A model he had built of the port of Liverpool came to the attention of the Canadian Pacific

136. A.C. Leighton
Sawback Range
Oil, 1953
24 1/4 x 30 1/4

137. A.F. Kenderdine
Top of the Hill
Oil, 1938
27 7/8 x 35 7/8

138. A.F. Kenderdine
Reflections
Oil, circa 1930
16 x 22

139. A.F. Kenderdine
The Marsh, Emma Lake
Oil, circa 1935
14 x 20

Railway, with the result that in 1924 he obtained the position of Chief Commercial Artist with the C.P.R. In this role he prepared numerous promotional brochures and other advertising forms, and also made a number of paintings of the Canadian West.

Leighton's first visit to the West was in 1925, followed by a more extensive trip in 1927. The arrangement with the C.P.R. was that they would pay all transportation costs and Leighton would pay his own living expenses. When he had completed a number of paintings, the company would have first selection, and those remaining could be exhibited and sold independently. During his second trip Leighton had a number of exhibitions in Canada and received very good reviews.

Leighton's interest in the West was sufficiently stimulated by his two trips that in 1929 he decided to move to Canada. He had been approached to become Director of Art at the Institute of Technology and Art in Calgary. His only teaching experience prior to this appointment had been as art master of the Dartford Art School for one year, in 1920. He accepted the Calgary position, and taught at the Institute until 1935; during this period, he played a major role in establishing it as a significant art school on the prairies.

As well as teaching full time at the Institute, Leighton started an art summer school in 1933. He sent letters to a number of students who he felt had promise, inviting them to the Kananaskis Ranch at Seebe, Alberta, to paint and draw for the summer. The school was held at the ranch for two summers and then the following year moved to Banff. However, Leighton's health failed after the third year and he was not able to continue. Nevertheless, an art summer school was instituted the next year as a part of the Banff School of Fine Arts, and has continued successfully since then.

Leighton belonged to a number of artistic societies, including the Royal Society of British Artists, the Royal Canadian Academy, and the Society for the Preservation of Windmills. He was also a founding member, in 1931, of the Alberta Society of Artists, which he believed important for communication among artists in the province.

Leighton would never display one of his own paintings in his house, although he did hang other paintings and prints, particularly Japanese pieces. His own personal work had to pass an inspection once a year; those that did not pass were discarded. Leighton had very strict and rigid standards for his own work and would not depart from them. Once his paintings passed his yearly test, he felt he could then exhibit or sell them.

Leighton would always do a sketch before breakfast, and then after eating spend the morning in the studio painting either scenes from the window, finished oils from preliminary sketches, or still-life subjects. The afternoon would be devoted to painting, a drive in search of a subject, brewing beer, or working in the greenhouse.

Leighton was an artist who liked to paint on location. He did not create subjects in his imagination, but insisted upon discovering a suitable real-life scene, usually in the mountains. If the light changed or for some reason a water colour could not be completed on the spot, it would remain unfinished. Leighton could spend two hours studying a scene, digesting the colour, form and composition, and then take as little as twenty minutes painting the picture.

While Leighton particularly excelled at water colour, and was most prolific with this medium, he also worked in oil. "Sawback Range" (Illustration No. 136) and "Above Timberline" (Illustration No. 144) both vividly show the majestic, almost cathedral quality of the mountains. In both paintings the mountains rise rapidly from the background, providing a backdrop for the landscape. The solidity of the mountains and rocks in the foreground can be seen in most of Leighton's oil paintings. Heavy emphasis is given to shadows to convey a real sense of plasticity. The texture of the paint, applied relatively thickly, reinforces the massiveness of the forms. The middleground has a tranquility and smoothness which forms a gentle transition from the ruggedness of the foreground to the rough vital forms of the mountains.

The colours of the two above-mentioned paintings are very subdued and subtle. Leighton's paintings are distinguished by their particular richness of tone, rather than the intensity of colour that characterizes the work of Phillips. Tonal variations in common hues provide an illumination of the rocks and water. The sunlight coming from the left highlights the right mountain and intensifies the cooler colours on the left mountain. On both mountains the same basic colours are used - it is Leighton's understanding of light that creates the atmosphere of the landscape.

"Floe Lake, Marble Canyon" (Illustration No. 1) has basically the same composition as the two previously mentioned Leighton oil paintings. The rocks are drawn in outline rather than as tight closed forms, and despite their indubitable

140. A.C. Leighton
View of Edmonton from the
North Saskatchewan River
Water colour, 1930
15 1/4 x 19 1/2

solidity, do not have the rugged textural quality of the rocks in the oil paintings. The elegantly simplified trees that stand above the rocks in the foreground are formed by smooth quick brushstrokes that convey a sense of lightness and freedom. Dominating the picture are the mountains, which are painted by delicate built-up layers of water colour that give both form and substance to the shapes. The result is not a precise record of each feature, but an overlay of brushstrokes and paint that convey the *feeling* of the mountain.

As with the oil paintings, light constitutes an important aspect of Leighton's water colours. In "Floe Lake, Marble Canyon", the sun is behind the mountains, casting a carefully pronounced shadow at the base. The clouds are small areas of colour that blend into each other. The effect of the translucent colour over the paper creates a softness to the clouds that contrasts with the massiveness of the mountain.

Leighton was very expressive at portraying the sky. In "View of Edmonton from the North Saskatchewan River"(Illustration No. 140) the sky is immense, extending from a point almost overhead and curving to the horizon. The landscape is relatively shallow, with the curve of the river pulling the viewer into the painting. While the buildings dot the horizon, it is the emphasis on space that is the dominant element of the water colour.

Leighton and W. J. Phillips are probably the two most impressive water-colourists of this period. Their ability with the medium was outstanding. Both artists conveyed a deep personal reaction to the environment. Phillips with his intense precise colours and expressive forms, and Leighton with his tonal subtlety and sense of space, created a unique imagery of the West.

The Rocky Mountains, and particularly Banff, have attracted many exceptional artists. Some came for the summers only, while others stayed throughout the year. Collectively, the work of the "Banff artists" forms an invaluable contribution to the total body of western Canadian art. One of these artists who gained an international reputation, especially as a natural history painter, was Carl C. M. Rungius.

Rungius was born near Berlin, Germany, in

141. Carl C.M. Rungius
Clearing in Wooded Foothill Country
Oil, no date
9 x 11

142. Carl C.M. Rungius
Brown Hillside
Oil, no date
9 x 11

143. Carl C.M. Rungius
Bush, Rock, Water and Mountain
Oil, no date
9 x 11

1869, the first child of the Reverend Heinrich and Magdalene Rungius. His grandfather, Gotthelf M. Rungius, collected and mounted birds, and was also a good animal artist, while his father was interested in conservation. It is no surprise then that from an early age Rungius was drawing and studying the outdoors and its natural inhabitants.

Rungius received regular schooling at the Gymnasium Magdeburg und Giessen. However, he was primarily interested in drawing and painting, and in 1889 attended the Berlin Art School. In the following years he studied at the Academy of Fine Arts and the School of Applied Arts in Berlin, where his ability at representing animals was cultivated. At the end of his first summer at the Academy, Rungius was awarded an Honorable Mention for animal painting, the highest award for a student. In the meantime, Rungius's father insisted that he learn the house-painting trade so that he could provide for himself.

In 1894 Rungius was invited by his uncle in Brooklyn, New York, to take a hunting trip to Maine. This was Rungius's first look at the country he was to adopt as his home. He decided to stay longer in the United States, and spent the ensuing summer hunting in Wyoming. Here Rungius fell in love with the West.

Rungius returned to Germany in 1896, only to realize that his enthusiasm for the country and the big game animals of the West had become too powerful to resist. He came back in 1897 to live at Greenpoint, on Long Island, New York. This was the location of his studio from 1897 to 1910, although the summers and falls were spent in Wyoming and New Brunswick, hunting and sketching. One year, 1904, was spent in the Yukon with Charles G. Sheldon, a noted naturalist and big game hunter.

From his early days in America to about 1902, Rungius sold illustrations to various magazines, such as *Everybody's*, *Outing*, and *McClure's*. Big game was the main subject of these illustrations.

The year 1910 was an important one for Rungius. He moved his studio from Greenpoint to New York, and there came into contact with eminent American artists such as Ben Foster, Gardner Symons, William Ritschel, and others. During the same year Rungius made his first visit to Alberta. He was so overwhelmed by the splendour of the Rockies that his whole approach to art changed: "For the first time I felt strongly the urge to paint straight landscape - that is, landscape for its own sake. Until then I had considered

144. A.F. Leighton
Above Timberline
Oil, no date
14 5/8 x 19 5/8

1. A. C. Leighton
Floe Lake, Marble Canyon
Water colour, 1930
14 5/8 x 18 1/2

145. Carl C.M. Rungius
Foothills, Valley and Mountain
Oil, no date
9 x 11

146. Carl C.M. Rungius
Tangle of Fallen Trees
Oil, no date
9 x 11

147. Carl C.M. Rungius
Green Field Landscape
Oil, no date
9 x 11

148. Carl C.M. Rungius
Winter
Oil, no date
9 x 11

149. Carl C.M. Rungius
Massive Rock Peak
Oil, no date
9 x 11

150. Carl C.M. Rungius
Top of Mountain
Oil, no date
8 3/4 x 11

151. Carl C.M. Rungius
Mountain Landscape
Oil, no date
9 x 11

152. Carl C.M. Rungius
Snowy Mountain Slopes
Oil, no date
9 x 11

153. Carl C.M. Rungius
Mountain Lake
Oil, no date
9 x 11

landscape only as a setting for big game animals. But the grandeur of the mountains with the marvelous atmospheric conditions in Alberta and consequent colour effects changed all of that."[7]

From that time on Rungius made annual pilgrimages to Alberta, until finally in 1921 he and his wife decided to build a studio in Banff. This became the base of his operations for further study of the Rocky Mountain country. Until 1958, a year before his death, Rungius spent his summers and falls at Banff, where he could fully explore and record the various animals and the landscape.

Rungius is primarily known as a natural history painter, and in this field he is considered one of the finest artists who ever lived. He did, however, paint a number of pure landscape paintings of the Rocky Mountains which are outstanding in their own right. He, like other artists in western Canada, liked to do sketches on location both in pencil and oil. His landscape oil sketches are relatively small in size, measuring approximately nine inches by eleven inches. He used his sketches both as study pieces and also as a basis for larger finished canvases.

The subjects of the sketches range from panoramic views to mountain tops to rock formations. In the oil sketches there is a freshness and spontaneity evident that captures both the power of the Rocky Mountains and the vitality of the artist. In "Mountain Side on a Cloudy Day"

154. Carl C.M. Rungius
Three Treetrunks and Boulders
Oil, no date
8 7/8 x 11

155. Carl C. M. Rungius
Unfinished Sketch
Oil, no date
9 x 11

156. Carl C.M. Rungius
Mountain Side on a Cloudy Day
Oil, no date
9 x 11

157. Carl. C.M. Rungius
Boulder Strewn Slope
Oil, no date
9 x 10 7/8

158. Carl C. M. Rungius
Deadfall and Autumn
Oil, no date
9 x 11

159. Belmore Browne
Spring Reflections
Oil, no date
18 x 24

160. Carl C.M. Rungius
High Country
Oil, no date
8 3/4 x 11

161. Belmore Browne
After September Snow
Oil, no date
20 x 23 7/8

(Illustration No. 156), the rock formations on the left seem to be chiseled in paint from the landscape. The powerful and massive qualities are immediately sensed. Rungius re-creates the essence of the rock without regard to a detailed, minute representation of every feature. The same can be said of "Massive Rock Peak" (Illustration No. 149) and "Snowy Mountain Slopes" (Illustration No. 152). The thick paint applied with a wide brush creates almost a sculptural quality. The brushstrokes are short and follow the outline of the rocks. The feeling imparted is that the artist has taken away segments of the mountain with his brush, not that he has applied paint to the canvas to build up the forms. There is nothing delicate or fragile about the sketches - they have a force and power that compel attention. In "Snowy Mountain Slopes" the dynamism of the mountain is emphasized by the strong diagonal line and emphasized again by the short brushstrokes.

This moulded quality so clearly evident in the rocks and mountains is equally apparent in the trees, foliage, and clouds. In "Tangle of Fallen Trees" (Illustration No. 146), "Foothills, Valley and Mountain" (Illustration No. 145), and "Mountain Landscape" (Illustration No. 151), the bare trees have a textural quality and a pronounced vertical line. Paint overlaps paint, segments blend into each other, creating highly *articulated* trees. Evergreens are short, almost random-placed brushstrokes of overlapping greens that provide substance and mass. Distant trees become a green carpet separated by a great illusionary space from the viewer.

The sky is painted in a similar manner. Brushstrokes are prominent, although usually less pronounced than the landscape itself. Occasionally clouds are formed by heavy application of paint, as in "Green Field Landscape" (Illustration No. 147), resulting in a pronounced plasticity, as if the clouds had been superimposed on top of the sky.

Rungius is not timid in his use of colour. A full range of tones is used, which vary with the seasons he is painting. The colours have the same sense of vitality as the shapes and forms. Rich ochres, blues, and green and yellow highlights all emphasize the brilliance actually found in the mountain landscape.

Rungius is undoubtedly one of the most significant painters of the western Canadian mountains. His understanding and his exceptional ability make them come alive in all their multiple forms and colours; he captures not only their image but their *character*. Perhaps more than any other artist of his time, Rungius succeeded in portraying the monumentality of the Rockies.

Another artist who spent prolonged periods of time in the Rocky Mountains was Belmore Browne. Like Rungius, Browne was fascinated by the mountain environment, and vividly portrayed it on numerous canvases.

Browne was born at Thompkinsville, Staten Island, New York, in 1880. In his childhood, the Browne family lived in Europe for several years. In 1888 or 1889 they travelled up the west coast of Canada and visited various places in Alaska, a visit Browne was to take many times in his life. After the trip to Alaska, Browne's father settled in Tacoma, Washington, and with two other men founded the St. Paul and Tacoma Lumber Company. Growing up in the Pacific Northwest, Browne developed a love for the outdoors and a skill for exploring and surviving under varying circumstances.

Browne attended various private schools in the eastern United States, spending his summers in the Washington state area. Although he was accepted at Harvard, due to family difficulties he could not attend. When he did return to school, instead of Harvard, Browne attended the New York School of Art. He also attended the Académie Julien in Paris.

In 1902 Browne joined his first expedition to the North, and began a career that was to last throughout his lifetime. For this expedition, sponsored by the American Museum of Natural History, he was signed on as artist, hunter, and specimen preparer. Browne made another trip the following year under the direction of the same explorer, Andrew J. Stone.

In 1906, in an expedition headed by Dr. Frederick A. Cook and Professor Herschel Parker, Browne made his first attempt to climb Mt. McKinley. The attempt was not successful, but the adventures of this and two subsequent climbs formed the basis of a book Browne published in 1913, *The Conquest of Mt. McKinley*. This was only one of the many books and articles he wrote about the North. He contributed articles to such magazines as *Collier's*, *Outing*, and *Hearst's*. During this period he also gave lectures on the North, particularly Alaska.

In 1921, Browne settled in Banff, Alberta, where he stayed until 1940. During this time he explored and painted numerous areas of the Rockies. For two years, 1934-36, while Banff was still his home, Browne was Director of the Santa

162. Belmore Browne
East Face of Black Douglas
Oil, no date
30 x 40 1/8

3. Belmore Browne
Under the Cliffs of Rundle
Oil, 1929
36 x 40

163. Belmore Browne
Mt. Hector
Oil, no date
18 x 24

164. Belmore Browne
Mountain Portal
Oil, 1946
25 x 30 1/8

Barbara School of the Arts in California.

With the outbreak of World War II, Browne served as an advisor both to the United States and England on survival and training in cold weather. He was to continue to advise and prepare manuals for the United States armed forces until about 1952, only two years before his death.

After the War, Browne once again moved back to Alberta, this time building a home on the Kananaskis River in Seebe. He stayed there until 1948.

In addition to his writing and painting, Browne also was well known for his natural history dioramas, which he prepared for a number of museums, including the American Museum of Natural History and the Boston Museum of Science.

Browne's paintings almost photographically capture the environment of the Rockies. As a rule they are extremely realistic, conveying the rich variety of forms and the cool colours of the mountains. He generally concentrated on panorama, and only very seldom on specific detail, in contrast to Rungius with his sketches.

In "Spring Reflections" (Illustration No. 159), a view of Mt. Rundle shows the clear, crisp definition of the landscape. Each form, from the blades of grass in the foreground to the mountain in the background, has a precise shape and colour that imparts total realism to the scene. "After September Snow" (Illustration No. 161) has the same characteristics, with the soft trees placed against the spectacular setting of Lake Louise. Browne characteristically used tight compositions that have an immediate foreground and an open middleground, with the mountains rising up across the back. This emphasis on a confined and limited space can be seen in both "Spring Reflections" and "After September Snow" as well as in most of his other works.

Both of the above paintings convey the feeling of the bright brilliant cold so unique to the mountains. At other times, the different mood of an overcast winter sky is created. In "Snowswept Cliffs" (Illustration No. 168), the dominant blue colour is still very evident, but is more subdued. The hazyness of the sky and distant mountains strongly suggest an oncoming storm.

Browne employed a similar technique to Rungius in the representation of rocks. The "cubic" treatment suggesting a feeling of massiveness is evident in "Mt. Hector" (Illustration No. 163) and "East Face of Black Douglas" (Illustration No. 162). The brushstrokes are used to build up the paint reinforcing the massive quality.

165. Belmore Browne
A Bend in the Bow River
Oil, no date
25 x 30 1/8

166. Belmore Browne
Clouds over Crowfoot Glacier
Oil, no date
25 x 30

Browne's paintings of the mountains are usually of views that could be seen by any visitor. He tried to portray what he saw without exaggerating or distorting. The result is an image based on experience and insight into the rugged mountain environment.

With artists such as W. J. Phillips, A. F. Kenderdine, A. C. Leighton, and Carl Rungius moving to western Canada and setting up their studios, the stimulus of cultural and artistic life was accelerated. Up until the end of the century, there were a number of professional artists who were intrigued with the West and recorded it, but it was not until artists actually settled in the West and lived there, to experience all the many facets of the western Canadian environment, that a real understanding developed.

These artists not only saw the land as a mosaic of images, but could show in their painting the essence of the environment, by exploiting every possibility of form, space, and colour. With them came a greater familiarity with the landscape, and from that a more profound understanding of its nature. Also with them came a teaching role, directly and indirectly, to a new generation of native-born artists.

167. Belmore Browne
Rising Clouds, Lake Louise
Oil, no date
16 x 20

168. Belmore Browne
Snowswept Cliffs
Oil, no date
25 x 30

170. Belmore Browne
Wilderness Waterfall
Oil, no date
40 x 30

169 Belmore Browne
Vermillion Lakes
Oil, no date
24 x 30

4. Contemporary Views

Overleaf:
171. I.H. Kerr
Ice and Still Water, Canmore
Oil, 1969
21 1/2 x 29 1/2

172. Emily Carr
Chemainus Bay
Oil, no date
13 1/4 x 17 3/4

The contemporary view of western Canada provides another dimension to the interpretation and understanding of the landscape. A higher degree of emotional response, and the desire to show more than pure images mark most of the art of the twentieth century. This characteristic, of course, is universally apparent, and does not occur exclusively or primarily in western Canada. Expressionism, in a general rather than a stylistic sense, becomes more important in the paintings.

Maxwell Bates, one of the foremost western Canadian artists of the contemporary period, wrote, "Experience gives me increased ability to transpose what I see. My intention is to transpose meaningfully. This amounts to expressionism, in my opinion. The meaning escapes description: it cannot be put in words. Design and colour are the techniques by which meaningful transpositions are made. I don't get enough satisfaction from exploiting them for their own sakes. That seems like empty theatrical gesticulation."[1]

The desire to interpret the land with a deeper, more profound insight than had ever been done before might well be considered the definitive quality of the contemporary artist within this genre.

The first truly significant artist born in western Canada is Emily Carr. Through her deep perception and desire to express the West Coast environment, she made a major contribution to a *cultural* understanding of the western landscape.

Emily Carr was born in Victoria, British Columbia, on December 13, 1871, and attended public and high school there. At the age of eighteen she left Victoria to attend the San Francisco School of Art. For the next five years, until 1895, Carr received her first real art instruction, and acquired a good basic technical knowledge of the subject.

Upon returning to Victoria, Carr set up a studio and began giving art lessons. It was also shortly after her return to Victoria that she made her first visit to the Indian villages at Ucluelet and other locations on the West Coast. This experience instilled a deep interest in the culture and art of various Indian tribes.

Carr at this point in her life was still strongly influenced by the European attitude which held the Canadian countryside as a subject for landscape painting in contempt:

Artists from the Old World said our West was crude, unpaintable. Its bigness angered, its vastness and wild spaces terrified them. Browsing cows, hooves well sunk in the grass (hooves were hard to draw!), placid streams with an artistic wriggle meandering through pastoral landscape - that was the Old World idea of a picture. Should they feel violent, the artists made blood-red sunsets, disciplined by a smear of haze. They would as soon have thought of making pictures of their own insides as of the depths of our forests.

I was tremendously awed when a real French artist with an English artist-wife came to Victoria. I expected to see something wonderful, but they painted a few faraway mountains floating in something hazy that was not Canadian air, a Chinaman's shack on which they put a curved roof like an Eastern temple, then they banged down the lids of their paintboxes, packed up, went back to the Old World. Canada had no scenery, they said. They said also that the only places you could learn to paint in were London or Paris.[2]

Not surprisingly, the moral authority exerted by the European traditions had a somewhat inhibiting effect on the artist's perceptions of her subject matter:

To attempt to paint the Western forests did not occur to me. Hadn't those Paris artists said it was unpaintable? No artist that I knew, no Art School had taught Art this size. I would have to go to London or to Paris to learn to paint. Still those French painters who had been taught there said, "Western Canada is unpaintable!" How bothersome! I nibbled at silhouetted edges. I drew boats and houses, things made out of tangible stuff. Unknowingly I was storing. Storing, all unconscious, my working ideas against the time when I should be ready to use this material.[3]

From her teaching Carr saved enough money to visit England, where she stayed from 1889 to 1904. While in England she attended the Westminster School of Art in London; participated in an art colony in St. Ive's, Cornwall; and studied at a school in Hertfordshire. However, her time in England was not entirely happy, as she became ill and had to spend about eighteen months in a sanitorium.

On her return to Victoria, Carr drew a number of cartoons for the newspaper *The Week*. In late 1904 or early 1905 she moved to Vancouver, where she gave art lessons, travelling in the summer to Indian Villages on the coast.

In 1910, Carr decided once again to visit

Europe, this time going to Paris to attend the Académie Colarossi. However, illness forced her to go to Sweden, where she recuperated. After returning to Brittany to paint for the spring and summer, she returned to Victoria in 1911. She tried to resume her teaching, but without success. She then moved to Vancouver for a year before settling permanently in Victoria in 1913.

In order to support herself she built a boarding house which was named "The House of All Sorts". The house, while it did bring some small income, was a source of continual worry and work. However, it provided material for one of her books by the same name, published in 1944, the year before her death.

The response to her painting, both from the public and the critics, was markedly unenthusiastic, and Carr had to endure an amazing barrage of ridicule and contempt:

In spite of all the insult and scorn shown to my new work I was not ashamed of it. It was neither monstrous, disgusting nor indecent; it had brighter, cleaner colour, simpler form, more intensity. What would Westerners have said of some of the things exhibited in Paris - nudes, monstrosities, a striving after the extraordinary, the bizarre, to arrest attention. Why should simplification to express depth, breadth and volume appear to the West as indecent, as nakedness? People did not want to see beneath surfaces. The West was ultra-conservative. They had transported their ideas at the time of their migration, a generation or two back. They forgot that England, even conservative England, had crept forward since then; but these Western settlers had firmly adhered to their old, old, outworn methods and, seeing beloved England as it had been, they held to their old ideals . . . . My pictures were hung either on the ceiling or on the floor and were jeered at, insulted; members of the "Fine Arts" joked at my work, laughing with reporters. Press notices were humiliating.[4]

Faced with such trenchant criticism of her work, Carr gave up painting between 1917 and 1928. During this period, however, her paintings came to the attention of the National Gallery of Canada in Ottawa. The result was an invitation to participate in the Exhibition of West Coast Art in 1927. This marked the beginning of national attention and recognition.

More important than the exhibition itself was the opportunity for Carr to travel to the East. There she met members of the Group of Seven as well as other artists who had a similar feeling and sense of the Canadian landscape. It was their encouragement, particularly that of Lawren Harris, that convinced her to begin painting once again. Shortly after she was visited by the well known American painter Mark Tobey, an event which provided a further impetus to her desire to return to painting.

From this time on Carr continued to paint, and gained an increasingly impressive reputation for her dramatic representations of the West Coast landscape and Indian cultures. She still made trips to various parts of British Columbia gathering ideas for her paintings. This close association and exploration of nature provided the essential inspiration for her work:

Indian Art broadened my seeing, loosened the formal tightness I had learned in England's schools. Its bigness and stark reality baffled my white man's understanding. I was as Canadian-born as the Indian but behind me were Old World heredity and ancestry as well as Canadian environment. The new West called me, but my Old World heredity, the flavour of my upbringing, pulled me back. I had been schooled to see outsides only, not struggle to pierce.

The Indian caught first at the inner intensity of his subject, worked outward to the surfaces. His spiritual conception he buried deep in the wood he was about to carve. Then - chip! chip! his crude tools released the symbols that were to clothe his thought - no sham, no mannerism. The lean, neat Indian hands carved what the Indian mind comprehended.

Indian Art taught me directness and quick, precise decisions. When paying ten dollars a day for hire of boat and guide, one cannot afford to dawdle and haver this vantage point against that.

I learned a lot from the Indians, but who except Canada herself could help me comprehend her great woods and spaces?[5]

Carr's paintings became more and more popular both in Canada and internationally. The year before her death, the Dominion Gallery in Montreal had an exhibition of sixty of her paintings; fifty-seven of them were sold. Beyond question, she gained public acceptance within her own lifetime, and a reputation that has continued to grow since.

Carr was also an exceptionally fine writer. *Klee Wyck*, a collection of sketches about Indian

173. Emily Carr
Winter Moonlight
Oil, circa 1910-12
34 1/2 x 22 1/4

174. Emily Carr
Landscape with Tree
Oil, circa 1912
21 1/4 x 17

175. Emily Carr
The Old Cypress
Oil, circa 1912
17 3/4 x 19 3/4

176. Emily Carr
Midsummer Eve
Oil, no date
16 5/8 x 22 3/4

177. Emily Carr
Clover Point, Victoria, B.C.
Oil, no date
22 1/4 x 34 1/2

178. Emily Carr
Autumn
Oil, circa 1912
17 1/2 x 19 1/2

180. Maxwell Bates
Road in the Foothills
Water colour, no date
10 x 17

179. Emily Carr
Among the Firs
Oil, circa 1930-40
36 x 30

181. W.L. Stevenson
Autumn Snow
Oil, no date
23 7/8 x 30

182. I. H. Kerr
Valley Road, Winter
Oil, 1928
10 x 12 1/8

4. I.H. Kerr
Barn with Stacks, Qu'Appelle Hills
Oil, 1929
18 7/8 x 24

192

culture, was published in 1941 and won the Governor General's Award. This publication was followed by *The Book of Small* in 1942, *The House of All Sorts* in 1944, and her autobiography, *Growing Pains*, published posthumously in 1946.

Carr's paintings, as they developed, assumed a stronger and stronger dynamic quality in portraying the essence of the environment. Her emotional understanding and reaction to the landscape gives her art an added dimension beyond the actual image itself.

"Winter Moonlight" (Illustration No. 173) is one of Carr's relatively early paintings. The lushness of the forest is vividly suggested by the closed-in composition in which trees and other foliage fill in the complete area of the canvas. The placement of the tree trunks carries the viewer into the painting, but a wall of green deliberately cuts off the feeling of real depth. While Carr is not primarily interested in detailed realism, there is a realistic sense of the landscape elements.

In "Autumn" (Illustration No. 178), Carr has begun to convey a greater feeling of energy than in "Winter Moonlight". Strong broad brushstrokes virtually carve the rocks in the foreground, creating plastic, almost movable forms. The rich greens, yellows, and reds add to the three-dimensional quality of the rocks. One tree rises up from the low point of the rocks, spreading out with spindly branches and curving dramatically to the left. Small dashes of various colours accent the tips of the branches, and emphasize the position of the tree at the left. Carr has brought the major subject matter close to the picture plane, but the landscape beyond - the hills, water, and the sky - while formed with the same strong brushstrokes, are painted in relatively subdued colours. The background therefore directs more attention to the immediate foreground.

Many of the same characteristics can be seen in "Landscape with Tree" (Illustration No. 174) and "The Old Cypress" (Illustration No. 175) Strong dynamic rocks accentuate the foreground which is built up by broad areas of paint. Curving thin trees that rise out of the rocks are pushed to one side by the wind. Carr conveys the *sense* of the windblown trees without itemizing them.

"Among the Firs" (Illustration No. 179), which was painted many years after "Winter Moonlight", is in many ways a similar composition to the earlier work. The difference in treatment of the elements within the composition, however, is remarkable. The trees now have a greater dynamism as they rise dramatically out of the ground. Instead of delicate areas of paint for the leaves, broad undulating bands wrap around the trees to form a complete blanket at the top of the painting. Instead of the gradual shift of the composition to the background, strong swirling lines agitate the middleground to pick up the lines of the foreground, thereby creating a more intense overall effect. The activity and inter-relationship of all the forms vividly impart a total energy to the painting.

"Clover Point, Victoria, B.C." (Illustration No. 177) has some of the same action and dynamism as "Among the Firs". Broad sweeping brushstrokes pull the water towards the shore; brushstrokes at a ninety degree angle push the sky up from the curve of the land. Carr then inter-relates the two forms by curved lines on the left half of the painting. There is a strong sense of movement, of wind tying the water and sea and sky together.

Carr in her paintings dramatically conveyed the energy of the West Coast environment. This was a personal understanding, an emotional reaction, which is almost unique in Canadian art. Her work now enjoys a national and international reputation - a reputation well deserved.

W. L. Stevenson was born in Guelph, Ontario, in 1905, and moved with his family to Calgary at the age of five. He received his early education in Calgary. Although he did study drawing under Lars Hawkaness at the Provincial Institute of Technology and Art in Calgary for a short period of time, he was chiefly self taught. He had an acute aesthetic sensitivity, and often was requested to provide criticism for fellow artists.

Stevenson exhibited at The Vancouver Art Gallery, the Edmonton Art Gallery, and the Royal Canadian Academy. He gained a certain reputation in Canada for his landscape paintings, but a significant recognition of his work did not come until 1963, when Clement Greenberg, the noted New York art critic and writer, wrote in an issue of *Canadian Art*, "My discovery among landscape painters was W. L. Stevenson, whose style does not suffer from its closeness to Goodridge Roberts. I had the good fortune to see a show of Stevenson's and can't understand why he is not known all over Canada."[6]

Stevenson painted in a very expressionistic style, totally captivated by the western landscape. "Autumn Snow" (Illustration No. 181) is typical of his oil paintings, a medium he preferred. Earthy colours are applied in a loose and fluid manner. Broad brushstrokes form the waving shape of the land gently diminishing into low grey hills in the background. The snow is applied very freely on the ground, not minutely constructed into banks or layers. A few black lines in the foreground and background applied to the yellow provide additional definition. The foliage and trees become very loose forms, with minimal brushstrokes shaping the trunk and branches, and broad areas of rich yellows, oranges, and reds creating the sense of leaves. Stevenson is attempting not only to convey a pictorial representation of the landscape, but also a feeling of its characteristic rough form and variety of colours. The texture of the paint is clearly evident, providing an additional plastic quality to the painting. The painting has a high degree of spontaneity to it, but has unquestionably been carefully thought out and constructed.

A contemporary and good friend of Stevenson in Alberta was Maxwell Bates. Born in 1906 in Calgary, Bates received his early education there. In 1924 he began to work in his father's architectural office, and in fact continued to practise architecture until 1961; one of his major buildings is St. Mary's Cathedral in Calgary, which he designed in the early 1950's with A. W. Hodges. Bates studied at the Provincial Institute of Technology and Art, Calgary, in 1926 and 1927. In order to expand his artistic scope he left Calgary in 1931 for England.

While in England Bates studied both painting and architecture, and earned his living at both professions, exhibiting regularly with the Twenties Group in London. In 1939 he joined the British Territorial Army, and as a member of the British Expeditionary Force landed at Le Havre in 1940. He was captured by the Germans the following year and was held a prisoner of war until 1945.

Bates returned to Calgary in 1946 and continued to paint and practise architecture. He taught in the Provincial Institute of Technology and Art in 1948 and 1949. In turn, he also studied at the Brooklyn Museum Art School under Max Beckman and Abraham Rattner in 1949 and 1950, after which he returned once again to Calgary.

Bates has gained an impressive reputation both for his paintings and for his architectural design. He has exhibited in numerous centres in Canada, the United States, and England, including the Royal Academy in London, the National Gallery of Canada, The Vancouver Art Gallery, and galleries in Chicago and Philadelphia.

Bates has always been predominantly interested in figure and social painting; a relatively small proportion of his output has been devoted to abstract art and to landscapes. The landscapes, however, have the same basic sense as his figure work: "I knew I wanted to do things simply and intensely and as directly as possible, and I've never changed from that idea."[7] All his paintings have a marked strength, with the well constructed and powerful forms conveying the essence of the subject.

Bates has a complete understanding of the surrounding environment and the people:

[Prairie families], that's a recurring subject . . . . You see, I've lived in Calgary - I guess Calgary isn't really the prairies, it's the foothills, really, but still it's enough of the prairies for me to have a feeling about the prairies. And I think I have a feeling for it . . . . the pioneers, and so on, the people of the early days . . . . a hard life, the soil and all that.

I've always done landscapes, always enjoyed it very much. I get a great deal of satisfaction from doing it . . . . I'm very pleased that the landscape painting is becoming popular again. And the Group of Seven, I think, has been thought too little of lately, because I think they're quite a good group of painters.[8]

"Summer Trees" (Illustration No. 183) and "Road in the Foothills" (Illustration No. 180) are typical of Bates's landscape work. "Road in the Foothills", a water colour, has a very simplified structure. Broad bands of colour create the low rolling hills; the variation in the colours emphasizes the depth of the landscape. The road in the centre is not a continuous straight line but is squared off and broken, with the diminishing width reinforcing the sensation of depth and distance. In comparison to the squared landscape forms, the sky is made up of broad areas of soft blue that stand in marked contrast to the rugged quality of the land. The partially finished trees on the right give a sense of scale to the foreground and to the rest of the painting.

"Summer Trees", an oil painting, has a very loose, fluid quality. On the left, broad brushstrokes form the trees; thinner, almost random brushstrokes form the branches, and dabs of paint provide articulation on the tree trunks. Careful brushstrokes in the foreground suggest additional foliage, although this is not clear. The landscape beyond is formed by areas of paint which become progressively less pronounced as they recede. While there is no emphasized sense of

perspective, the depth is made clearly evident by means of the colour and the paint itself. There is a strong feeling of spontaneity and freedom in the painting, a feeling for the landscape without an attempt to record every element in its known form.

Stevenson and Bates have interpreted the western foothills in distinctly different ways. Stevenson, with deep earth colours expressing a sense of the land, fluidly presents the variety and freedom of the elements. Bates, on the other hand, simplifies the environment to provide a clear, concise statement of his artistic vision. A third artist in Alberta, Illingworth Kerr, has assumed another attitude. Illingworth Kerr is considered by some commentators to be the most expressive painter ever to depict the prairie landscape. Maxwell Bates wrote in an exhibition catalogue in 1963, "Few painters have been closer to the Prairie than Illingworth Kerr. He knows the Prairie as few painters have . . . ."[9]

Born in Lumsden, Saskatchewan, in 1905, Kerr had an early interest in drawing animals, and received some technical training from his mother. After he finished high school, he travelled to Toronto to study art at the Central Technical School and then at the Ontario College of Art from 1924 to 1927. Arthur Lismer, J.E.H. MacDonald, Frederick Varley, and J. W. Beatty

183. Maxwell Bates
Summer Trees
Oil, no date
13 5/16 x 17 3/8

184. I.H. Kerr
Muskeg at Night
Oil, 1932
20 x 24

were among his instructors. While the "style" of the Group of Seven was not taught, Kerr had an opportunity to view paintings by this new group of artists at various exhibitions and in studio visits to A. Y. Jackson and Lawren Harris. Their work had a great impact on Kerr. "It became my ambition to paint the prairie country in the same spirit as these artists had painted other parts of Canada, seeing it with the eyes unprejudiced by European influences."[10]

In 1927 Kerr returned to Lumsden to work at his painting, as well as at other jobs which were necessary in order to earn a living. He gained some recognition through exhibitions, although there were very few sales. The isolation in which he worked was reinforced by the Depression, and Kerr's attempt at being a professional artist was disappointing. Nevertheless he was determined to create a body of art that would encompass a total interpretation of the prairies:

Since the Group of Seven had passed up the prairies I thought someone should do something about it. The mistake was taking to the prairies only the equipment to deal with concrete form. The problem of space was not to be dealt with in terms of pattern. Lineal design dissolved in perspective. A straight horizon line pinching back to infinity became a dominating tyrant. I was painfully aware that realism (the literal aspect of nature) must throttle the prairie artist. Space, however, seemed incompatible with the means at my disposal. More recently it has challenged me to attempt abstract equations. In the Dirty Thirties our environment was too personal, too malignant a force, to become so disembodied.[11]

Kerr was well aware of the need to work in the company of other artists in order to obtain a more meaningful critical insight into his approaches to art. With this in mind, he worked his passage aboard a cattle boat to England in 1936. While in England, he attended the Westminster School of Art, worked on films, and wrote short stories for *Blackwood's Magazine*. The association with *Blackwood's Magazine* was to continue through 1945. He also published *Gay Dogs and Dark Horses*, a collection of Canadian short stories, which appeared in 1946, as well as turning out illustrations for a number of other Canadian books.

Kerr returned to Canada in 1943 and settled in Vancouver, where he was employed as a production illustrator for Boeing Aircraft. His career as an art teacher began in 1945 at the Vancouver School of Art. He spent two years there before coming to Calgary in 1947 to direct the Art School of the Provincial Institute of Technology and Art. With his guidance, the Art School developed over a twenty-year period into a significant and influential college.

Kerr has received a number of honours, including a senior Canada Council Fellowship in 1960 and an honorary doctorate from the University of Calgary in 1973, which was awarded partly in recognition of his outstanding teaching career in Alberta.

The western landscape and western animals have always been the basic subject matter of Kerr's painting. "I still painted landscape and was thrilled by Calgary's proximity to mountains, foothills and prairie. The latter still eluded me and there loomed the hope that ABSTRACT was the answer to Western space with its vast scale, its power of mood rather than tangible forms. So I went to the great advocate of abstract expressionism, Hans Hofmann. The experience was as challenging as hoped for but I never did successfully apply my new insights into interpretation of the great flat land."[12] While Kerr's paintings do have a sense of abstraction, the majority of the landscapes are not abstract in the real sense of the word.

In "Valley Road, Winter" (Illustration No. 182), Kerr uses the texture of the paint to add to the multi-faceted quality of the landscape. The paint is particularly built up on the tops of the hills where the light is hitting, thereby emphasizing their curvature and shape. As such, the hills are smooth soft forms, without a high degree of articulation. The same is true of the bushes and trees, which become bands of vertical colour, opaque in their treatment. The rhythm of the landscape is subtle, with a short foreground and then a slight curving of the trees picked up by the hills as they stretch to the horizon.

Many of the same characteristics are evident in the painting "Barn with Stacks, Qu'Appelle Hills" (Illustration No. 4). Soft flowing curves make up the snow formations, the straw stacks, and the hills beyond. Even the barn on the right, which normally would be a hard crisp outline, seems soft in its shape. As in "Valley Road, Winter", the sense of depth is gradual, with each part of the painting flowing into the next. There is a sense of the land, with only minimum emphasis given to the quality of engulfing space.

In "Straw Stacks, March Thaw" (Illustration No. 188), Kerr vividly illustrates the distance and colour of the prairies. Once again the soft gently curved lines are used to form the ground with the almost marshmallow-textured straw stacks rising up from the snow. The colour of the land is subdued in comparison to the brilliantly coloured mosaic of the sky. Yellows, reds, greens, and blues instantly strike the viewer with their intensity. The broad brushstrokes used to apply the paint to the canvas give an energy and plasticity to the sky. The painting has the forceful, almost overwhelming quality of the prairie panorama.

"The Arbutus Trees, Saanich, B.C."(Illustration No. 189) is another strongly visual and colourful painting. The ground, branches, and leaves are a multiplicity of colours, almost abstract in their form. Rich intense purples, oranges, greens, and reds inter-relate forming a two-dimensional screen with hints of a blue background. Everything is brought close to the picture plane so that the highest degree of design and colour is evident. In terms of these qualities, the painting does become an abstraction of nature, even though the basic outline of the recognizable images is still present.

"Ice and Still Water, Canmore (Illustration No. 171), a mountain landscape, differs from Kerr's earlier prairie landscapes by the use of more rectangular forms. The mountains have sharp, clearly defined outlines, as does the ice in the foreground lake, in contrast to the smooth curving hills of the prairies. The mirror image of the mountains in the lake is sharply divided from the actual mountains themselves by a horizontal band of dark colour. Like "Straw Stacks, March Thaw" or "Barn with Stacks, Qu'Appelle Hills", the composition is extremely tight. Kerr studies and interprets the specific scene carefully to contain it within the framework of the painting. As with all his art the intent is not to pull the viewer into the painting or focus the attention on one aspect, but instead to concentrate on the rhythm of a composition that provides an inter-relationship of parts forming an integrated total. The result is a panoramic view in which every component of the composition has approximately the same importance.

Kerr's paintings are strong statements of the prairies and mountains. Rich colours and soft,

185. Illingworth Kerr
Spring Break-Up
Oil, 1962
28 x 38

186. James McL. Nicoll
River with Towering Cliffs
Pen and black ink, 1961
12 x 9

187. James McL. Nicoll
Landscape of Castor Creek Area
Pen and black ink, 1961
16 x 20

often elegant forms show the poetry and rhythm of the western environment. The complementary qualities of colour, form, and space create a total image that is exciting and perceptive.

James McL. Nicoll, another Alberta artist, was born at Fort Macleod in 1892. Nicoll attended the University of Alberta, graduating with a degree in engineering. He worked for the Canadian Pacific Railway for many years.

Nicoll did not begin as a painter until 1935, but since then has continued to portray the environment and history of the West. As such he was largely self-taught, although he spent two years, 1958 and 1959, at the Art Students League in New York. However, his training as a civil engineer undoubtedly prepared him for his painting and drawing. "Well, I'm a civil engineer and therefore trained as a professional draftsman and I study minutely and in detail. While I'm painting trees, I'm continuously studying the trees that appear out here under various light conditions and I draw the way the limbs come out and the texture of the bark and I also insist on structure - as an engineer. I insist on structure and the value of line as a function of form."[13]

Nicoll, like Kerr, provided illustrations for books, and in addition was the founding editor of *Highlights*, a magazine put out by the Alberta Society of Artists. This magazine, which included both descriptive articles and original works, became an important cultural organ in Alberta.

Nicoll has always had a very basic attitude towards his work. "Yes, I paint what I like. Every artist is supposed to have a philosophy - I have no philosophy; I just paint what I like. I have certain ground rules which I have acquired through study and experience and they operate more or less sub-consciously so that I am constantly exhilarated and excited by nature, especially living out here - our clouds and our rivers and our trees and all the rest of it. I'm interested psychologically more than anything in contemporary trends, but abstract art is dehumanized and I'm a humanist philosophically and my rules - I wouldn't dignify them by the name of philosophy - they're just ground rules. It's just as simple as that; I paint what I like."[14]

Two ink drawings by Nicoll, which were done on an archaeological field trip in 1961, vividly demonstrate his interest in the logical structuring of composition and his technical skill at draftsmanship. "River with Towering Cliffs" (Illustration No. 186) is a compact composition showing a multiplicity of line. Parallel cross-hatching and

188. I. H. Kerr
Straw Stacks, March Thaw
Oil, 1935
30 1/4 x 36 3/4

189. I.H. Kerr
The Arbutus Trees, Saanich, B.C.
Oil, 1968
11 1/2 x 15 1/2

191. Dorothy Knowles
Down to the River
Oil, 1973
53 x 59 1/2

190. Joseph Plaskett
Badlands, Drumheller, Alberta
Pastel, 1968
18 3/4 x 24

192. Wynona Mulcaster
Prairie Snow
Oil, 1960
30 x 48

193. D. Otto Rogers
Spring Thaw
Acrylic, 1973
60 x 60

194. Robert Sinclair
Sunset Time
Pencil and water colour, 1973
5 5/8 x 7 1/2

195. Robert Sinclair
Cloudy Buildup
Pencil and water colour, 1973
7 5/8 x 5 1/2

196. Robert Sinclair
Road Shadow
Pencil and water colour, 1973
13 x 9 3/4

198. Robert Sinclair
Stacked Road
Pencil and water colour, 1971
7 3/4 x 5 1/2

197. Robert Sinclair
Great Canadian Landscape: Dusky Road
Plastic, 1971
7 x 7 x 8 1/2

207

199. Harlan House
Sunny Alberta
Ceramic and cloth, 1973
93 x 42

short lines all combine to create the visual texture. Instead of filling in the images with ink, Nicoll achieves a more evocative effect by carefully leaving areas of white paper: for instance, some trees are outlined, while others are filled in. Nicoll simplifies the landscape while including all its major elements.

The drawing "Landscape of Castor Creek Area" (Illustration No. 187) conveys a sense of detail even though not every element of the scene is recorded. For instance, the trees in the background are again a combination of positive and negative shapes creating a dense forest. The rock cliff on the left is depicted by small irregular black areas that provide definition to the cliff face. The creek is a solid black form that clearly divides the landscape and leads the eye into the drawing.

In both drawings, as in most of Nicoll's art, there is a strong sense of pattern evident. A variety of lines and shapes and contrasting rich black and white areas are used to build up the landscape. The result is invariably a remarkable combination of artistic economy and bold forcefulness and power.

Another contemporary Alberta artist who has a particular interest in landscape painting is J. Stanford Perrott. Born in Claresholm, Alberta, in 1917, Perrott studied painting at a number of institutions including the Provincial Institute of Technology and Art in Calgary, the Banff School of Fine Arts, the Pennsylvania Academy of the Fine Arts, and the Art Students League, New York. He has lived and worked almost exclusively in Alberta, first as instructor at the Alberta College of Art in Calgary and then as the Head of the same school.

Perrott's paintings of the prairies and foothills are usually done in water colour. "Cold Saturday" (Illustration No. 200) and "Prairie Fence Line" (Illustration No. 201) are both in this medium. Flat opaque colours are used to build up the various landscape elements. In both water colours, Perrott represents a large amount of ground with only minimal attention given to the sky. In "Cold Saturday" the starkness of a winter day is vividly portrayed. The only articulation against the smooth whiteness of the snow is the spindly forms of the snow fence in the foreground and the fence posts and wire towards the back. By giving emphasis to the horizontal quality of the painting and by diminishing the scale, a sense of depth is created.

"Prairie Fence Line" is painted with overlapping layers of opaque white and light blue that build up the textural quality of the snow. The road on the left seems flat until it reaches the fence lines; it then recedes rapidly to the horizon. Once again the sky is a small band with no sense of articulation. "Prairie Fence Line", like "Cold Saturday", conveys a barren, isolated quality, and the coldness and stillness of the winter landscape.

"Badlands, Drumheller, Alberta" (Illustration No. 190) conveys the same harsh qualities seen in the previous two works. This pastel is by Joe Plaskett, who was born in New Westminster, B.C. in 1918 and now lives in Paris. After graduating from the University of British Columbia in 1939, Plaskett taught history at the high school level. He also attended the Vancouver School of Art and later the California School of Fine Arts and the Slade School, London. He turned from teaching history to teaching art, and from 1947 until 1949 was Principal of the Winnipeg School of Art.

In 1949 Plaskett left for Europe for two years, and finally in 1951 settled in Paris, where he has continued to live. He makes frequent trips to Canada, however, and "Badlands, Drumheller, Alberta" was done on one of these visits. This drawing presents a partial panoramic view of the desolate and rugged features of the Badlands. Short quick lines create various hills and cliffs; no attempt is made to represent every element of the scene, but only sufficient details to provide the image without making it photographic. The brown coloured paper sets the general tone, and the dark colours articulate the shapes. The resulting impression Plaskett gives of the Badlands is predominantly romantic.

The prairies have produced a number of significant painters who used the landscape as a source for their work. Wynona Mulcaster was born in Prince Albert, Saskatchewan, in 1915. Upon graduating from the University of Saskatchewan she received a degree in English. She then turned to art and studied at a number of institutions and under a number of well known artists, including A. F. Kenderdine at Emma Lake; Henry Glyde and A. Y. Jackson at the Banff School of Fine Arts; Arthur Lismer at the Montreal School of Art and Design; and Ernest Lindner, with whom she studied privately. Her training provided not only a strong technical background but also a definite basis for interpretation, as all of these artists expressed a deep interest in the landscape.

Two of her oil paintings, "Evening" (Illustration No. 202) and "Prairie Snow" (Illustration No. 192) express particularly well the essence of the prairies without itemizing every detail. The broad

200. J.S. Perrott
Cold Saturday
Water colour, 1963
20 7/8 x 28 5/8

areas of colour applied loosely in "Prairie Snow" overlap and form a visually heavy-textured quality. The ground becomes a pattern of flat planes of irregular shapes that meet the deeply blue sky. There is a strong sense of energy, spontaneity, and vitality to the painting conveyed both by the colours and the shapes. The only real hints of specific landscape elements are the thin vertical lines on the left which suggest trees. The rugged sensual response to the prairies is clearly evident.

The same can be said of "Evening". Once again loose broad brushstrokes apply the paint in a deceptively random fashion, to provide a dynamism and energy to the painting. One can sense the heavier emphasis on building forms in the foreground and the receding of the landscape to the gently curved horizon line. The sky, like the ground, is built up by free brushstrokes. The trees on the right simultaneously seem three-dimensional and flat, but are nevertheless sufficiently clear that the landscape does not become completely abstract.

These two paintings by Mulcaster are abstractions of the prairie landscape, but only in the sense of images. The rugged, vital energy of the prairies is clearly understood and vividly portrayed. The result is a strongly emotional statement about the prairie environment.

Another Saskatchewan artist who has a deep understanding of the prairies is D. Otto Rogers. A native of Saskatchewan, Rogers was born at Kerrobert in 1935. After attending Saskatchewan Teachers' College, he went to the University of Wisconsin, receiving an M.A. in Fine Arts. Currently Rogers is Head of the Department of Art of the University of Saskatchewan.

Rogers's acrylic paintings are relatively large, ranging in size from five feet by five feet to five feet by eight feet. "Spring Thaw" (Illustration No. 193), like his other paintings, is characterized by an overwhelming sense of immense space, tranquility, and mystery. Soft subtle colours in delicate bands along the lower part of the painting indicate a sense of the land. These are intersected by other lines that provide articulation and reinforce the picture plane. The sky occupies the major part of the canvas. Soft gentle tones, ever so slightly changing from blues to browns, give a feeling of space and at the same time a sense of depth. The clouds, portrayed with a more opaque colour than the sky, have a looseness and decrease in size as they approach the horizon. As with the lower part of the painting, where there is a sense of receding space, the sky also has a feeling of

201. J. S. Perrott
Prairie Fence Line
Water colour, 1963
21 1/4 x 28 3/4

depth, yet at the same time the visible texture of the canvas gives the viewer the sensation of surface *and* depth. The small black areas at the three edges of the painting, which at first may seem unnecessary, serve to annunciate the edges themselves and provide terms of reference for the frame of the composition.

Rogers's paintings, like Mulcaster's, vividly illustrate a feeling for and of the prairies. While Mulcaster was conveying their energy and vitality, Rogers conveys their peacefulness and space. His work is an abstraction of visually identifiable forms, instead of a literal interpretation of the environment.

Dorothy Knowles, another Saskatchewan painter, has the same sensitivity about the prairie landscape as Rogers and Mulcaster. Born in Unity, Saskatchewan, in 1927, she studied art at the University of Saskatchewan under Eli Bornstein; at the Banff School of Fine Arts; and at the Emma Lake Artists' Workshops under Clement Greenberg, Kenneth Noland, and Jules Olitski. Since the early 1960's, she has exhibited extensively in Canada and is represented in practically every major art gallery in this country.

The primary subject matter for Knowles's paintings is the western Canadian landscape, especially that of the prairie region. An excellent example of her approach is "Down to the River", (Illustration No. 191) a relatively large (53 inch by 59½ inch) oil painting. The work has an immense sensation of depth and space. The viewer is partially looking down on the prairie scene as it stretches dramatically towards the horizon. The foliage is built up carefully, with yellows and browns forming light, airy, loosely defined patterns, although there is no suggestion of photographic exactness. Soft subdued colours and gentle forms add to the tranquility of the painting. This effect is heightened by Knowles's technique of thinning the oil paint until it lies almost transparently on the canvas. The river quietly meanders throughout the middleground of the painting, tying together all the landscape elements. The soft blue of the sky augments the feeling of space achieved by the painting as a whole. Despite the large scale, there is the intimacy of a smaller work. The painting is a very personal interpretation of the landscape that shows the subtle qualities of the prairies.

The work of Robert Sinclair comprises a unique image of the western Canadian landscape. Sinclair was born in Saltcoats, Saskatchewan, in 1939. After receiving a B.F.A. degree from the University of Manitoba in 1962, he attended the University of Iowa, graduating with an M.A. and then an M.F.A. He taught art at high school, and currently is on the staff of the Department of Art and Design, University of Alberta, Edmonton.

Sinclair's pencil and water-colour paintings are small, delicate interpretations of the landscape. The features are kept to a minimum, as is the colour, so that the viewer is compelled mentally to fill in the spaces himself, by his own intimate familiarity with the subject. In "Road Shadow" (Illustration No. 196), Sinclair makes no attempt to use the full size of the paper. A pronounced, totally clear highway recedes sharply into the distance, with pencil lines forming gently rolling hills on either side. The clouds seem almost on a string attached to the horizon line. The use of line, while minimal, creates a complete landscape. Watercolour is only used at one location in the foreground, with just enough colour to enable the viewer to complete the painting in his own imagination.

Basically the same treatment is evident in "Cloudy Buildup" (Illustration No. 195). Colour is implied as well as actually used. The sense of sky is very strong, with the three tiers of billowing clouds. The immensity of the prairies has been vividly captured.

In "Stacked Road" (Illustration No. 198), Sinclair concentrates more on the land than on the sky. A road defined by three lines curves over low rolling hills. The hills in the background are formed both by pencil outline and solid water colour. Trees in the middleground are shown in various green colours; once again, Sinclair has used a pencil line to suggest more trees in front of the painted ones. The great sense of depth of the previous two paintings is again evident. Sinclair seems to edit the landscape in order to form negative and positive spaces; despite this technique - or perhaps because of it - the paintings are so strongly done that the totality of the landscape is never in doubt.

Sinclair does not limit his landscape art to the two-dimensional piece of paper. "Great Canadian Landscape: Dusky Road", for example (Illustration No. 197), is a three-dimensional plastic sculpture. This is a relatively new and experimental form. A road winds through a cloud into a literally remote distance. The same softness of the cloud forms seen in the water colours is repeated here. Gently curved outlines and delicately twisted forms overlap to create a compact composition. Again, a similar sense of positive and negative

202. Wynona Mulcaster
Evening
Oil, 1960
48 x 30 1/2

203. Robert Sinclair
Sunset
Pencil and water colour, 1973
5 5/8 x 7 1/2

space is achieved by cutting out part of the plastic or leaving areas without any colour.

The feeling of space and the exploration of forms in Sinclair's water colours and sculptures show an understanding of the prairie environment that is unique. For reasons of both interpretation and innovation, Sinclair merits an important place in the contemporary understanding of western landscape art.

Another artist who uses a medium not generally associated with the landscape is Harlan House. Although born in Vancouver, House was raised on the Alberta prairies. He studied art and ceramics at the Alberta College of Art, and subsequently organized a studio with two other ceramists under the name "The Clay Association". In the spring of 1973 he moved to Ontario to set up a new studio.

"Sunny Alberta" (Illustration No. 199) is a clay and canvas landscape. The landscape is comprised of textured bands which recreate the image of the prairies when the fields are being ploughed. The wide and heavy rays of a small sun shoot out from the horizon, while thick moulded clouds rest on the landscape. The compositional elements overlap, although there is no real attempt to create a sense of retreating space. A protruding tongue made from segments of black painted canvas pinned together thrusts the colour of the ground out to the viewer. The result is a light-hearted, innovative, almost humorous treatment of the landscape.

The western Canadian landscape has been studied and painted by innumerable artists and in innumerable styles and manners of interpretation. The contemporary artists have drawn upon the iconography of the western environment and presented it as a very personal and expressive image. Each has abstracted from the landscape a particular theme or emphasis, and dramatically conveyed it in his own fashion. Emily Carr presented the energy, movement, and dynamism of the West; Stevenson suggests the rich feeling of the earth; while Bates illustrates the simple geometry of land forms. Kerr with his intense colours and strongly constructed undulating forms presents one view of the prairies, while Rogers implies a peaceful and calm image that is an almost total contrast. A similar if less pronounced difference can be seen between Knowles's subtlety of form and colour, and Sinclair's freedom of form and space. Each of these artists has interpreted the landscape in a very personal and individual sense, and by so doing, has enlarged the potential depth of understanding with which the non-artist can appreciate the beauty of the land itself.

Throughout the history of art the landscape has been an integral part of painting, but initially, it was as a secondary element of a larger composition. It was not until the early nineteenth century that the landscape assumed an important role, and artists began studying and interpreting it as a subject in its own right. Even though a great awareness quickly developed as such notable figures as John Constable, Claude Monet, and Paul Cézanne extended the inherent possibilities of the landscape far beyond any previous understanding, the history of the genre is relatively short. Indeed, landscape painting as a pure form is scarcely older than some of the earliest representations of western Canada included in this book.

Practically from the time of its discovery, there has been a deep artistic interest and response to the western countryside. Unquestionably this is due to the extraordinary nature of a land that demanded attention and respect so convincingly. The artists represented in *The Mountains and the Sky*, in responding to the environment have provided numerous and varied records, from romantic to formalized, from idyllic to passionate, from naturalistic to abstract. The artist has acted as an interpreter, to help or even compel a more sensitive insight into the innumerable elements, moods, scenes, and other qualities that make this land so beautiful.

REFERENCE NOTES

INTRODUCTION.

1. James G. MacGregor, *Behold the Shining Mountains; being an Account of the Travels of Anthony Henday, 1754-55, the First White Man to Enter Alberta* (Edmonton: Applied Arts Products, 1954), p. 64.

2. _____, *Peter Fidler: Canada's Forgotten Surveyor 1769-1822* (Toronto: McClelland and Stewart, 1966), p. 66.

3. Sir A. Mackenzie, *Journals and Letters of Sir A. Mackenzie*, Edited by W. Kaye Lamb (Cambridge: Cambridge University Press, 1970), p. 265.

4. The Earl of Southesk, *Saskatchewan and the Rocky Mountains A Diary and Narrative of Travel, Sport, and Adventure, During a Journey Through the Hudson's Bay Company's Territories in 1859 and 1860* (Edinburgh: Edmonston and Douglas, 1875), p. 178.

5. Ibid, pp. 178-79.

6. W. H. Williams, *Manitoba and the North-West A Journal of a Trip from Toronto to the Rocky Mountains* (Toronto: Hunter, Rose, 1882), p. 123.

7. Wallace Stegner, *Wolf Willow A History, a Story, and a Memory of The Last Plains Frontier,* (New York: The Viking Press, 1962), p. 7.

8. T. B. Higginson, "Moira O'Neill in Alberta", *Alberta Historical Review,* Vol. V, No. 2 (Spring, 1957), pp. 23-24.

CHAPTER 1.

1. Paul Kane, *Wanderings of an Artist among the Indians of North American from Canada to Vancouver Island and Oregon through Hudson's Bay Company's Territory and back Again* (Edmonton: m.g. hurtig ltd., 1968), p. 1xii.

2. James Berton Rhoads, "When the Wild Northern Boundary Stretched to the Sea a Government Artist Recorded the Rugged Surveying Job", *American Heritage,* Vol. VIII, No. 4 (June, 1957) p. 15.

3. Letter from R.B. Nevitt to My Dear S... from Belly River, October 11th, 1874.

CHAPTER 2.

1. Edgar Andrew Collard, "All Our Yesterdays — Historic Painting Exhibited by V.O.N.", (Montreal; *Gazette* November 3rd, 1962), n.p.

2. P. Turner Bone, *When the Steel Went Through* (Toronto: MacMillan, 1947), p. 79.

3. J. Russell Harper, *Painting in Canada A History* (Toronto: University of Toronto Press, 1966), p. 196.

4. William Colgate, *Canadian Art Its Origin and Development* (Toronto: The Ryerson Press, 1943), pp. 32-33.

5. W. Wilfred Campbell and T. Mower Martin, *Canada* (London: A. & C. Black, 1907), pp. ix and 9.

6. Letter from Mrs. A.C. Mackie, Toronto, to Glenbow, August 28th, 1960, Glenbow Art Department.

7. Anonymous, "Mountain Sketches", (Winnipeg: *Free Press,* October 18th, 1887), p. 4.

8. Ibid, p. 4.

9. L. Rombout, *John Hammond, R.C.A. 1843 — 1939* (Sackville: Owens Art Gallery, Mt. Allison University, 1967), n.p.

10. Ibid, n.p.

11. Gladys Christina McDonald, "Early Scenes from Western Canada", *Canadian Geographical Journal,* Vol. XIII, No. 3 (July, 1936), p. 119.

12. Franz Stenzel *Cleveland Rockwell, Scientist and Artist, 1837-1907* (Portland: Oregon Historical Society, 1972), p. 73.

CHAPTER 3.

1. John Bruce Cowan, *John Innes Painter of the Canadian West* (Vancouver: Rose, Cowan and Latta Limited, 1945), p. 9.

2. Duncan Campbell Scott, *Walter J. Phillips* (Toronto: The Ryerson Press, 1947), pp. 22 and 24.

3. Walter J. Phillips, *Above Lake Louise* (Alexandria, Virginia: Woodcut Society, 1945), n.p.

4. Eckhardt, Ferdinand, *H. Eric Bergman Memorial Exhibition,* (Winnipeg: Winnipeg Art Gallery, 1960-61), n.p.

5. Ibid, n.p.

6. Arthur Hayworth, "James Henderson of the Qu'Appelle Valley", *Saskatchewan History,* Vol. XI, No. 2. (Spring, 1958) p. 61.

7. W. J. Schaldack, *Carl Rungius, Big Game Painter* (Vermont: Countrymen Press, 1945), pp. 81-82.

CHAPTER 4.

1. Maxwell Bates, Introduction by Ronald Bloor, *Maxwell Bates Retrospective Exhibition* (Regina: Norman Mackenzie Art Gallery, 1960-61), n.p.

2. Emily Carr, *Growing Pains The Autobiography of Emily Carr* (Toronto: Oxford University Press, 1946), p. 103.

3. Ibid, p. 107.

4. Ibid, p. 306.

5. Ibid, p. 283.

6. Clement Greenberg, "Clement Greenberg's View of Art on the Prairies: Painting and Sculpture in Prairie Canada Today", *Canadian Art,* Vol. XX, No. 2 (March, April, 1963) p. 100.

7. Maxwell Bates, *Maxwell Bates in Retrospect 1921-1971* (Vancouver: Vancouver Art Gallery, 1973), p. 13.

8. Ibid, p. 23.

9. Maxwell Bates, *Illingworth Kerr Exhibition,* (Edmonton: Edmonton Art Gallery, 1963), n.p.

10. I. H. Kerr Interview, November 1962, Glenbow Art Department.

11. I. H. Kerr, *Illingworth Kerr: Fifty Years a Painter* (Calgary: Alberta College of Art, 1973), n.p.

12. Ibid, n.p.

13. Interview with J. McL. Nicoll by Helen K. Wright, January 29th, 1973, Glenbow Art Department.

14. Ibid.

BIBLIOGRAPHY

BOOKS

Baker, Marcus. *Survey of the Northwestern Boundary of the United States 1857-1861.* Washington: Government Printing Office, 1900.

Bell, Michael. *Painters in a New Land.* Toronto: McClelland and Stewart, 1973.

Bone, P. Turner. *When the Steel Went Through.* Toronto: MacMillan, 1947.

Butler, Sir William Francis. *The Great Lone Land.* London: Sampson Low, 1872.

Campbell, W. Wilfred, and Martin, T. Mower. *Canada.* London: A. & C. Black, 1907.

Carr, Emily. *Klee Wyck.* Toronto: Oxford University Press, 1941.

_____. *The Book of Small.* Toronto: Oxford University Press, 1942.

_____. *The House of All Sorts.* Toronto: Oxford University Press, 1944.

_____. *Growing Pains.* Toronto: Oxford University Press, 1946.

Colgate, William. *Canadian Art Its Origin and Development.* Toronto: The Ryerson Press, 1943.

Cowan, John Bruce. *John Innes Painter of the Canadian West.* Vancouver: Rose, Cowan and Latta Limited, 1945.

Deutsch, Herman J. "A Contemporary Report on the 49° Boundary Survey", in Herman J. Deutsch, ed., *Surveying the 49th Parallel, 1858-61.* Tacoma: Washington State Historical Society, 1962.

Dilworth, Ira. *Emily Carr Her Paintings and Sketches.* National Gallery of Canada and Art Gallery of Toronto. Toronto: Oxford University Press, 1945.

Duval, Paul. *Canadian Water Colour Painting.* Toronto: Burns and MacEachern, 1954.

Grant, George Monro (ed.). *Picturesque Canada The Country as It Was and Is.* 2 Vols. Toronto: Belden Bros., 1882.

Harper, J. Russell. *Painting in Canada A History.* Toronto: University of Toronto Press, 1966.

_____. *Early Painters and Engravers in Canada.* Toronto: University of Toronto Press, 1970.

_____. *Paul Kane's Frontier* including *Wanderings of an Artist Among the Indians of North American* by Paul Kane. National Gallery of Canada, Ottawa, and Amon Carter Museum, Fort Worth. Austin: University of Texas Press, 1971.

Hubbard, R. H. *An Anthology of Canadian Art.* Toronto: Oxford University Press, 1960.

_____. *The Canadian School.* (Catalogue of Paintings, Vol. III). Toronto: University of Toronto Press, 1960.

Josephy, Alvin M. Jr. *The Artist was a Young Man The Life Story of Peter Rindisbacher.* Fort Worth, Texas: Amon Carter Museum of Western Art, 1970.

Kane, Paul. *Wanderings of an Artist among the Indians of North America from Canada to Vancouver Island and Oregon through the Hudson's Bay Company's Territory and Back Again.* Reprinted edition. Edmonton: m.g. hurtig ltd., 1968.

Kennan, George. *Siberia and the Exile System.* Vol. I & II. New York: The Century Company, 1891.

_____. *Tent Life in Siberia A New Account of an Old Understanding, Adventures among the Koraks and other Tribes in Kamchatka and Northern Asia.* New York: G.P. Putnam's Sons, 1910.

Kerr, Illingworth H. *Gay Dogs and Dark Horses.* Toronto: J.M. Dent and Sons (Canada) Ltd., 1946.

Mackenzie, Sir A. *Journals and Letters of Sir A. Mackenzie.* Edited by W. Kaye Lamb. Cambridge: Cambridge University Press, 1970.

MacGregor, James G. *Behold the Shining Mountains; being an Account of the Travels of Anthony Henday, 1754-55, the First White Man to enter Alberta.* Edmonton: Applied Arts Products, 1954.

_____. *Peter Fidler: Canada's Forgotten Surveyor 1769-1822.* Toronto: McClelland and Stewart, 1966.

Nevitt, R. B. *A Winter at Fort Macleod.* Edited by Hugh A. Dempsey. Calgary: McClelland and Stewart West/Glenbow-Alberta Institute, 1974.

Phillips, W. J. *The Technique of the Colour Woodcut.* New York: Brown-Robertson, 1926.

Phillips, Walter J., and Niven, Frederick. *Colour in the Canadian Rockies.* Toronto: Thomas Nelson and Sons Ltd., 1937.

Reid, Dennis. *A Concise History of Canadian Painting.* Toronto: Oxford University Press, 1973.

Robson, Albert H. *Canadian Landscape Painters.* Toronto: The Ryerson Press, 1932.

Roper, Edward. *By Track and Trail A Journey Through Canada with Numerous Original Sketches by the Author.* London: W.H. Allen and Co. Ltd., 1891.

Schaldack, W. J. *Carl Rungius, Big Game Painter.* Vermont: Countryman Press, 1945.

Scott, Duncan Campbell. *Walter J. Phillips.* Toronto: The Ryerson Press, 1947.

Southesk, the Earl of. *Saskatchewan and the Rocky Mountains A Diary and Narrative of Travel, Sport, and Adventure, During a Journey Through the Hudson's Bay Company's Territories in 1859 and 1860.* Edinburgh: Edmonston and Douglas, 1875.

Spendlove, F. St. G. *The Face of Early Canada.* Toronto: The Ryerson Press, 1958.

Stegner, Wallace. *Wolf Willow A History, a Story, and a Memory of the Last Plains Frontier.* New York: The Viking Press, 1962.

Stenzel, Franz. *Cleveland Rockwell Scientist and Artist, 1837-1907.* Portland: Oregon Historical Society, 1972.

Taft, Robert. *Artists and Illustrators of the Old West.* New York: Charles Scribner's Sons, 1953.

Walbran, Captain John T. *British Columbia Coast Names 1592-1906 to Which are Added a Few Names in Adjacent United States Territory Their Origin and History with Map and Illustrations.* Ottawa: Government Printing Bureau, 1909.

Williams, W. H. *Manitoba and the North-west A Journal of a Trip from Toronto to the Rocky Mountains.* Toronto: Hunter, Rose, 1882.

EXHIBITION CATALOGUES

Allison, Carlyle. *The Art of W. J. Phillips, Artist and Teacher.* Winnipeg: Hudson's Bay Company, 1970.

Balkind, Alvin. *Joe Plaskett and His Paris — In Search of Time Past.* Vancouver: Fine Arts Gallery, University of British Columbia, 1971.

Bates, Maxwell. *Maxwell Bates in Retrospect 1921-1971.* Vancouver: The Vancouver Art Gallery, 1973.

_____. *Illingworth Kerr Exhibition.* Edmonton: Edmonton Art Gallery, 1963.

Bell, Michael. *Image of Canada.* Ottawa: Public Archives of Canada, 1972.

Bloore, Ronald. *Maxwell Bates Retrospective Exhibition.* Regina: Norman Mackenzie Art Gallery, 1960-61.

Crabb, John P. *Graphics by Walter J. Phillips, R.C.A., LL.D.* Calgary: Glenbow-Alberta Institute, 1968.

Eckhardt, Ferdinand. *H. Eric Bergman Memorial Exhibition.* Winnipeg: Winnipeg Art Gallery, 1960-61.

BIBLIOGRAPHY (cont.)

_____. *H. Eric Bergman*. Winnipeg: Winnipeg Art Gallery, 1969.

_____. *150 Years of Art in Manitoba*. Winnipeg: Winnipeg Art Gallery, 1970.

Ediger, E. P. *A. F. Kenderdine*. Calgary: Glenbow-Alberta Institute, 1968.

Ferguson, Bruce W. *A Prairie Sweet*. Calgary: Glenbow-Alberta Institute, 1973.

Kerr, I. H. *Fifty Years a Painter*. Calgary: Alberta College of Art, 1973.

Oko, Andrew. *The Frontier Art of R. B. Nevitt*. Calgary: Glenbow-Alberta Institute, 1974.

Phillips, Walter J. *Above Lake Louise*. Alexandria, Virginia: Woodcut Society, 1945.

Render, Lorne E. *An Artist's View of Nature: Carl Rungius*. Edmonton: Provincial Museum and Archives of Alberta, 1969.

_____. *A. C. Leighton*. Calgary: Glenbow-Alberta Institute, 1971.

Rombout, L. *John Hammond, R.C.A. 1843-1939*. Sackville: Owens Art Gallery, Mount Allison University, 1967.

Shadbolt, Doris. *Emily Carr. A Centennial Exhibition Celebrating the One Hundredth Anniversary of her Birth*. Vancouver: The Vancouver Art Gallery, 1971.

Shuebrook, Ron. *Otto Rogers*. Calgary: Glenbow-Alberta Institute, 1973.

Stanton, James B. *Impression of an Age*. Occasional Paper Number 1. Vancouver: Centennial Museum, 1969.

Wilkin, Karen. *Dorothy Knowles*. Edmonton: Edmonton Art Gallery, 1973.

Wowk, Stephanie. *James Henderson 1871-1951*. Saskatoon: Mendel Art Gallery, July, 1969.

PERIODICALS

Ayre, Robert. "Eric Bergman", *Canadian Art*, Vol. XV No. 3 (Summer 1958), 190-91 & 223.

Farrington, Lawrence. "H.M.S. Beaver", *The Beaver*, Spring 1961, 44-47.

Greenberg, Clement. "Clement Greenberg's View of Art on the Prairies: Painting and Sculpture in Prairie Canada Today". *Canadian Art*, Vol. XX No. 2 (March-April 1963), 90-107.

Hayworth, Arthur. "James Henderson of the Qu'Appelle Valley", *Saskatchewan History*, Vol. XI No. 2 (Spring 1958), 59-66.

Higginson, T. B. "Moira O'Neill in Alberta", *Alberta Historical Review*, Vol. V No. 2 (Spring 1957), 22-24.

Hudson, Andrew. "Nonie Mulcaster on the Western Canada Art Circuit", *Canadian Art*, Vol. XIX No. 6 (Nov.-Dec. 1962), 395.

Kennedy, Michael S. "Belmore Browne and Alaska", *The Alaska Journal*, Vol. 3 No. 2 (Spring 1973), 96-104.

Mackay, Corday. "The Collins Overland Telegraph", *British Columbia Historical Quarterly*, Vol. X No. 3 (July 1946), 187-215.

McDonald, Gladys Christina. "Early Scenes from Western Canada", *Canadian Geographical Journal*, Vol. XIII No. 3 (July 1936), 115-25.

Neesham, Robin. "W. L. Stevenson at the Calgary Allied Arts Centre", *Canadian Art*, Vol. XX No. 5, (Sept.-Oct. 1963), 270.

Patterson, H. S. "54° 40' or Fight", *The Beaver*, June 1936, No. 1, 38-44.

Pettus, Terry. "Expedition to Russian American", *The Beaver*, Winter 1962, 8-19.

Rhoads, James Berton. "When the Wild Northern Boundary Stretched to the Sea a Government Artist Recorded the Rugged Surveying Job", *American Heritage*, Vol. VIII, No. 4, (June 1957), 15.

NEWSPAPERS

Anon. "Feels Fame for Him Lies Beyond Grave, John Hammond, Noted Landscape Artist, Realizes Painter Must Die Ere Work Really Valuable". Edmonton: *Journal*, Nov. 24, 1928.

Anon. "Grand Old Man of Canadian Art Possesses a Fine Record". Calgary: *Herald*, Mar. 1, 1924.

Anon. "Mountain Named for Artist". Calgary: *Albertan*, June 13, 1970.

Anon. "Mountain Sketches". Winnipeg: *Free Press*, Oct. 18, 1887.

Collard, Edgar Andrew. "All Our Yesterdays — Historic Painting Exhibited by V.O.N." Montreal: *Gazette*, Nov. 3, 1962.

Greenaway, C. Roy. "Nestor of Canada's Artists Still Wields Brush at 91. John Hammond, R.C.A. Disciple of Millet and Whistler". Calgary: *Herald*, Dec. 23, 1933.

Pintarich, Paul. "Early Oregon Scenes Depicted by Engineer". Portland: *Oregonian*, April 20, 1972.

LIST OF WORKS

	Illus.	Page
JAMES M. ALDEN		
Kishinena Pass	10	24
MAXWELL BATES		
Road in the Foothills	180	190
Summer Trees	183	195
F. M. BELL-SMITH		
Glacier Stream, Selkirks, B.C.	36	47, 60
Morning, Lake Louise	51	62
Mt. Baker from Oak Bay, Victoria, B.C.	63	73
H. ERIC BERGMAN		
Strange Rock Formations	74	89
Snow Scene	111	120
Burned-over Trees	112	121
Oaks and Wind	113	122
Fir Tree in Snow	114	123
Approaching Storm	115	124
Waterfall	116	125
Trees	117	125
Sunlight on Trees	118	126
Little Sand Lake, Minaki	119	126
The Jackpine	121	129
Trees by Water	122	130
SARA MARY BLAKE		
Falls on the Middle Fork of Old Man's River	75	90
GEORGE S. BRODIE		
Sunset, Metlaskatla	11	24
Mt. Baker, Washington Territory	12	27
Lowe Inlet	13	28
Needle Peak on the Portland Inlet	14	29
Sunset, Lambert Channel, Vancouver Island	15	30
McLaughlin Upper Lake	16	30
View from the Anchorage, Nanaimo	29	41
Seymour Narrows from the North	30	41
Entrance to the Nass River	31	41
BELMORE BROWNE		
Under the Cliffs of Rundle	3	12, 172
Spring Reflections	159	168
After September Snow	161	170
East Face of Black Douglas	162	172
Mt. Hector	163	173
Mountain Portal	164	174
A Bend in the Bow River	165	175
Clouds over Crowfoot Glacier	166	176
Rising Clouds, Lake Louise	167	177
Snowswept Cliffs	168	178
Vermillion Lakes	169	179
Wilderness Waterfall	170	179

	Illus.	Page
EMILY CARR		
Chemainus Bay	172	182
Winter Moonlight	173	185
Landscape with Tree	174	186
The Old Cypress	175	187
Midsummer Eve	176	188
Clover Point, Victoria, B.C.	177	189
Autumn	178	189
Among the Firs	179	190
ARTHUR P. COLEMAN		
Mt. Robson	37	49
JOHN D. CURREN		
Sinclair Canyon	76	91
Johnson's Canyon	77	92
Mt. Rundle, Banff	78	93
C.P.R. Tracks	79	94
The Barrier on the Kananaskis River	80	94
Winter Scene	81	95
LEONARD M. DAVIS		
Harvesting, Nobleford	55	64
Mountain Landscape, Bow Valley	73	86
EARL OF DUNMORE		
Souris River	7	20
Côteau des Prairies	8	21
THOMAS W. FRIPP		
Mt. Fairview from Mt. Temple	104	112
GEORGE A. FROST		
Mt. Baker	17	31
Falls at Nicoamen, Thompson River, B.C.	18	32
Trutch's Bridge, Chapman's Bar, Fraser River	19	32
The Great Cañon	20	33
Suchalet Lake, B.C.	21	34
Cascade Range	22	35
Scene near Nanaimo, Vancouver Island	32	42
JOHN HAMMOND		
The Three Sisters	50	62
Coldstream Ranch	64	74-75
Canadian Rockies, Banff	65	76
JAMES HENDERSON		
Qu'Appelle Valley I	123	131
Qu'Appelle Valley II	124	132

LIST OF WORKS (cont.)	Illus.	Page
HARLAN HOUSE		
Sunny Alberta	199	208
JOHN INNES		
Battle of the Rocks	82	96
PAUL KANE		
Buffalo Reposing near Sturgeon Creek	6	19
The Encampment, Rocky Mountains	9	22-23
A. F. L. KENDERDINE		
The Road in the Valley	120	128
Trees and Lake	125	133
The Valley in Winter	126	134
Windswept	127	135
Autumn on the North Saskatchewan	128	136
Sutherland Trail	129	137
Near Beaver Creek	130	138
Emma Lake Spruce	131	139
A Bit of Prairie	132	140
Emma Lake	133	140
Cutting the Road into Murray Point	134	141
On the Front, Murray Point	135	142
Top of the Hill	137	145
Reflections	138	146-47
The Marsh, Emma Lake	139	148
ILLINGWORTH KERR		
Barn with Stacks, Qu'Appelle Hills	4	15, 192
Ice and Still Water, Canmore	171	181
Valley Road, Winter	182	192
Muskeg at Night	184	196
Spring Break-Up	185	198
Straw Stacks, March Thaw	188	201
The Arbutus Trees, Saanich, B.C.	189	202
DOROTHY KNOWLES		
Down to the River	191	203
A. C. LEIGHTON		
Floe Lake, Marble Canyon	1	9, 154
Sawback Range	136	144
View of Edmonton from the North Saskatchewan River	140	150
Above Timberline	144	153
HERBERT B. LEWIS		
Mountain Range	38	50-51
Landscape 1886	39	52
Mountain Landscape near Golden, B.C.	40	53
Landscape	41	54

	Illus.	Page
T. MOWER MARTIN		
Landscape with Boat	43	57
Landscape	44	58
Train in the Mountains	46	59
Trial Island from near Victoria	56	65
At Howe Sound near Vancouver, B.C.	57	66
Rocky Mountains	58	67
The Bow River from the Banff Hotel	59	67
Arrow Lakes, B.C.	60	68
MARMADUKE MATTHEWS		
Twin Mountain Peaks	2	11, 69
Mt. Burgess	45	58
Monarch of the Selkirks	47	61
Valley of the North Kicking Horse, B.C.	48	61
Solitary Pine	49	61
South Bank of the Bow River near Laggan	61	70
Puffing Billy	62	72
WYNONA MULCASTER		
Prairie Snow	192	204
Evening	202	213
R. B. NEVITT		
Valley of the South Fork, Old Man's River	5	17
Second Crossing of the Souris	23	36
Below Falls, Bow River	24	37
Old Man's River (1876)	25	38
Camp on the Prairies	26	38
Rocky Mountains from Fort Calgary	27	39
Old Man's River (1875)	28	40
Lundbreck Falls	33	43
Mountain Landscape	34	44
The Porcupine Hills	35	45
JAMES McL. NICOLL		
River with Towering Cliffs	186	199
Landscape of Castor Creek Area	187	200
LUCIUS R. O'BRIEN		
Puget Sound	42	55
J. S. PERROTT		
Cold Saturday	200	210
Prairie Fence Line	201	211

LIST OF WORKS (cont.)

W. J. PHILLIPS

	Illus.	Page
Landscape	89	105
Lake Kalamalka	90	105
Vapours Round the Mountain Curled	91	106
Landscape	92	106
Landscape	93	106
Landscape	94	107
Landscape	95	107
Wenkchemna Pass	96	108
Waterfall	97	108
Saskatchewan Glacier	98	109
Landscape	99	109
Landscape	100	110
Peachland, Lake Okanagan	101	110
Assiniboine and Quartz Mountains	102	110
Blue Douglas Fir, Banff	103	111
Rundle through a Screen of Poplars	105	113
Lake of the Woods	106	114
Landscape	107	115
Howe Sound	108	116
Mountain Torrent	109	117
Leaf of Gold	110	118

JOSEPH PLASKETT

	Illus.	Page
Badlands, Drumheller, Alberta	190	203

THEODORE J. RICHARDSON

	Illus.	Page
Scene in British Columbia 52 63	52	63

CLEVELAND ROCKWELL

	Illus.	Page
Grenville Channel, B.C.	53	63
Banff Springs Hotel	54	63
The Inland Passage, B.C.	67	78
Glacier on Frederick Sound, Alaska	68	80
Harrison Lake, B.C.	69	81
Looking Down the Inlet, near Juneau	70	82-83

D. OTTO ROGERS

	Illus.	Page
Spring Thaw	193	205

EDWARD ROPER

	Illus.	Page
Mt. Field and Mt. Stephen	66	77

CARL C. M. RUNGIUS

	Illus.	Page
Clearing in Wooded Foothill Country	141	151
Brown Hillside	142	152
Bush, Rock, Water and Mountain	143	152
Foothills, Valley and Mountain	145	155
Tangle of Fallen Trees	146	156
Green Field Landscape	147	157
Winter	148	158
Massive Rock Peak	149	159
Top of Mountain	150	160
Mountain Landscape	151	161

CARL C. M. RUNGIUS (cont.)

	Illus.	Page
Snowy Mountain Slopes	152	162
Mountain Lake	153	162
Three Treetrunks and Boulders	154	163
Unfinished Sketch	155	164
Mountain Side on a Cloudy Day	156	165
Boulder Strewn Slope	157	166
Deadfall and Autumn	158	167
High Country	160	169

GEORGE HORNE RUSSELL

	Illus.	Page
Kicking Horse Pass	71	84
Roche Miette, Jasper National Park	72	85

CHARLES H. SCOTT

	Illus.	Page
The Winding River Fraser	83	98
A West Coast Rain	84	99
The Mighty Fraser	85	100
Mountains and Lake Garibaldi	86	101

ROBERT SINCLAIR

	Illus.	Page
Sunset Time	194	206
Cloudy Buildup	195	206
Road Shadow	196	206
Great Canadian Landscape: Dusky Road	197	207
Stacked Road	198	207
Sunset	203	214

W. L. STEVENSON

	Illus.	Page
Autumn Snow	181	191

INA D.D. UHTHOFF

	Illus.	Page
Glacier and Moraine	87	102
Castle Mountain	88	103

INDEX

"A West Coast Rain" — 98
Aberdeen Art School — 83
Aberdeen, Lord and Lady — 74
"Above Timberline" — 149
Académie Colarossi — 71, 184
Académie Julien — 87, 128, 171
Academy of Fine Arts (Berlin) — 152
"After September Snow" — 175
Alberta College of Art (Calgary) — 209, 215
Alberta Society of Artists — 149, 200
Alden, James M. — 13, 26, 28, 32, 38, 45
Alma College (St. Thomas, Ontario) — 71
Alpine Club — 87
American Museum of Natural History — 171, 175
"Among the Firs" — 193
"Approaching Storm" — 127
"Arrow Lakes, B.C." — 68
Art Association of Montreal — 56
Art Gallery of Greater Victoria — 101
Art Students League (New York) — 87, 200
"Autumn" — 193
"Autumn on the North Saskatchewan" — 143
"Autumn Snow" — 193
Ayre, Robert — 120

"Badlands, Drumheller, Alberta" — 209
Banff School of Fine Arts — 104, 149, 209, 211, 212
"Banff Springs Hotel" — 79
"Barn with Stacks, Qu'Appelle Hills" — 197
Barr Colonists — 140
Barraud, Cyril — 104
Bates, Maxwell — 13, 183, 194, 195, 215
"Battle of the Rocks" — 97
Beatty, J. W. — 195
Beckman, Max — 194
Bell-Smith, F. M. — 56, 71-73, 83
"Below Falls, Bow River" — 38
Bergman, H. Eric — 120, 124, 127
Berlin Art School — 152
Blackwood's Magazine — 197
Blake, Sara Mary — 90, 94, 97
"Blue Douglas Fir, Banff" — 114
Bone, P. Turner — 48, 55
Book of Small, The — 193
Bornstein, Eli — 212
Boston Museum of Science — 175
Bourne College (Quinton, Birmingham) — 104
Brassey Institute (Hastings, England) — 143
Breslau University — 48
Brigden, Fred — 120
British Columbia Society of Artists — 98
Brodie, George S. — 13, 18, 26, 28, 38, 45
Brooklyn Museum Art School — 194
Browne, Belmore — 171, 175
"Buffalo Reposing near Sturgeon Creek" — 25
"Burned-over Trees" — 124
By Track and Trail — 76

Calgary Herald — 97
California School of Fine Arts — 209
"Camp on the Prairies" — 45
Campbell, D. G. — 87
Campbell, W. W. — 68
Canada — 68
Canadian Art — 193
Canadian Illustrated News — 18, 37, 38, 71
Canadian National Railway — 83
Canadian Pacific Railway — 13, 48, 68, 73, 76, 83, 143, 149, 200
Canadian Rockies, The — 48

Carr, Emily — 13, 101, 183, 184, 193, 215
"Castle Mountain" — 101
Catlin, George — 18
Central Ontario School of Art — 68
Central Technical School (Toronto) — 195
Century Magazine — 30
Cézanne, Paul — 215
Chunks of the Western Epic — 97
Clay Association — 215
"Cloudy Buildup" — 212
"Clover Point, Victoria, B.C." — 193
"Cold Saturday" — 209
"Coldstream Ranch" — 74
Coleman, Arthur P. — 48
Colgate, William — 56
Collier's Magazine — 171
Collins Overland Telegraph — 28
Conquest of Mt. McKinley, The — 171
Constable, John — 215
Cook, Frederick A. — 171
"Côteau des Prairies" — 25
Curren, John D. — 90, 94, 97

Daily Colonist — 101
Dartford Art School (England) — 149
Davis, Leonard M. — 87, 97
Denby, Arthur P. — 97
Dominion Gallery (Montreal) — 184
"Down to the River" — 212
Dufferin Military Academy — 97
Dunmore, Earl of — 25, 28, 30, 38, 45, 56

"East Face of Black Douglas" — 175
Edmonton Art Gallery — 193
Elementary Geology — 48
Emma Lake Artists' Workshop — 140, 212
Epic of Transportation — 97
Epic of Western Canada — 97
"Evening" — 209
Everybody's — 152

"Falls on the Middle Fork of Old Man's River" — 90
Fidler, Peter — 10
"Floe Lake, Marble Canyon" — 150
"Foothills, Valley and Mountain" — 171
Foster, Ben — 152
Fripp, George Arthur — 97
Fripp, Thomas W. 97, 98
"From Trail to Rail" — 97
Frost, George A. — 13, 18, 30, 32, 38, 45

Gay Dogs and Dark Horses — 197
"Glacier and Moraine" — 104
"Glacier Stream, Selkirks, B.C." — 72
Glasgow School of Art — 98
Glyde, Henry — 209
Gravesend, Charles Storm de — 73
"Great Canadian Landscape: Dusky Road" — 212
"Green Field Landscape" — 171
Greenberg, Clement — 193, 212
"Grenville Channel, B.C." — 79
Grob, Trautman — 50
Group of Seven — 98, 197
Growing Pains — 193
Gyles, William — 104
Gymnasium Magdeburg und Giessen — 152

Hammond, John — 73, 74, 76, 83
Harris, Lawren — 184
Harrison, Alexander — 71
"Harrison Lake, B.C." — 79

"Harvesting, Nobleford" — 87
Hawkaness, Lars — 193
Hayworth, Arthur — 127
Hearst's Magazine — 171
Hellmouth College (London) — 97
Henday, Anthony — 10
Henderson, James — 127, 128
Highlights — 200
Hodges, A. W. — 194
Hofmann, Hans — 197
House, Harlan — 215
Hornet, The — 97
House of All Sorts, The — 184, 193
"Howe Sound" — 119

Ice Ages, Recent and Modern — 48
"Ice and Still Water, Canmore" — 198
Innes, John — 97, 98

Jackson, A. Y. — 197, 209
"Johnson's Canyon" — 94
Julien, Henri — 37

Kane, Paul — 13, 18, 25, 26, 28, 32, 38, 45
Kenderine, A. F. L. — 128, 140, 143, 176, 209
Kennan, George — 30
Kerr, Illingworth — 13, 195, 197, 198, 200, 215
"Kicking Horse Pass" — 83
King's College (Sherbourne, England) — 97
"Kishinena Pass" — 26
Klee Wyck — 184
Knowles, Dorothy — 212, 215

Lafosse, Chevalier — 128
"Landscape of Castor Creek Area" — 209
"Landscape with Tree" — 193
"Leaf of Gold" — 119
Lee, Sydney — 104
Legros, Alphonse — 83
Leighton, A. C. — 13, 143, 149, 150, 176
Lewis, Herbert B. — 48, 55
Lindner, Ernest — 209
Lismer, Arthur — 195, 209
"Lowe Inlet" — 28
Lorne, Marquis of — 11, 56
Louisianna Purchase Exhibition — 74
"Lundbreck Falls" — 38

MacDonald, J.E.H. — 195
Macdonald, J.W.G. — 98
MacKenzie, Sir Alexander — 10
Macleod, Col. James — 38
Manchester School of Art — 128
March West (of N.W.M.P.) — 32
Martin, T. Mower — 56, 66, 71, 73
"Massive Rock Peak" — 171
Matthews, Marmaduke — 56, 71, 73
McClure's — 152
Millet, François — 73
Monet, Claude — 215
Montreal School of Art and Design — 209
"Morning, Lake Louise" — 73
Mount Allison Ladies College (Sackville, New Brunswick) — 74
"Mt. Baker" — 30
"Mt. Baker from Oak Bay, Victoria, B.C." — 72
"Mt. Baker, Washington Territory" — 26
"Mt. Fairview from Mt. Temple" — 98
"Mt. Field and Mt. Stephen" — 76
"Mt. Hector" — 175
"Mt. Robson" — 48
"Mt. Rundle, Banff" — 94

Mountain Echoes — 97
"Mountain Landscape" — 45
"Mountain Landscape" — 171
"Mountain Landscape, Bow Valley" — 87
"Mountain Landscape near Golden, B.C." — 55
"Mountain Range" — 55
"Mountain Side on a Cloudy Day" — 162
"Mountain Torrent" — 119
Mounted Police *see* North West Mounted Police
Murray, Charles Adolphus *see* Dunmore
Mulcaster, Wynona — 13, 209, 211

National Gallery of Canada — 184, 194
National Gallery (Washington) — 74
Nevitt, R. B. — 13, 18, 37, 38, 45
New York School of Art — 171
Nicoll, James Mc L. — 200
Noland, Kenneth — 212
North West Mounted Police — 18, 37, 38
Notman, Photographers — 73

"Oaks and Wind" — 124
O'Brien, Lucius R. — 56, 73
"Old Man's River" — 38
Olitski, Jules — 212
O'Neill, Moira — 14
Ontario College of Art — 195
Ontario Society of Artists — 56, 72, 74
Outing — 152, 171
Owen's Art Institution (Saint John, New Brunswick) — 74

Pacific Coast Pilot — 79
Pacific Monthly — 79
Pan-American Exhibition (Buffalo) — 74
Paris Salon Exhibition — 74
Parker, Herschel — 171
Pennsylvania Academy of the Fine Arts — 209
Perrott, J. S. — 209
Phillips, W. J. — 13, 104, 114-20, 124, 127, 150, 176
Picturesque Canada — 56, 71
Plaskett, Joseph — 209
Portland Art Club — 79
"Prairie Fence Line" — 209
"Prairie Snow" — 209
Provincial Institute of Technology and Art (Calgary) — 193, 194
"Puget Sound" — 56

"Qu'Appelle Valley I" — 128
"Qu'Appelle Valley II" — 128

Rattner, Abraham — 194
"Reflections" — 143
Reid, Sir George — 83
Richardson, Theodore J. — 79
Richardson, T. M. — 71
Rindisbacher, Peter — 18
Ritschel, William — 152
"River with Towering Cliffs" — 200
"Road in the Foothills" — 194
"Road Shadow" — 212
Roberts, Goodridge — 193
"Roche Miette, Jasper National Park" — 83
Rockwell, Cleveland — 79, 83
"Rocky Mountains from Fort Calgary" — 38
Rogers, D. Otto — 13, 211, 212, 215
Roper, Edward — 76, 79
Royal Academy — 56, 104, 194
Royal Academy Art School — 97

Royal Academy of Belgium — 30
Royal Canadian Academy — 48, 56, 71, 72, 74, 83, 149, 193
Royal Society of British Arts — 149
"Rundle through a Screen of Poplars" — 114
Rungius, Carl C. M. — 13, 150, 152, 162, 171, 175, 176
Russell, George Horne — 83, 87, 97

St. John's Wood Art School (Winnipeg) — 97
St. Mary's Cathedral — 194
Santa Barbara School of the Arts — 171
San Francisco School of Arts — 183
Saskatchewan Teachers' College — 211
"Sawback Range" — 149
"Scene in British Columbia" — 79
School of Applied Arts (Berlin) — 152
School of Practical Science (Toronto) — 48
Scott, Charles H. — 98, 101, 104
Scott, Duncan Campbell — 114
Seaby, Allen W. — 104
Sheldon, Charles G. — 152
Simpson, Sir George — 18
"Sinclair Canyon" — 94
Sinclair, Robert — 13, 212, 215
Slade School (London) — 209
"Snow Scene" — 127
"Snowswept Cliffs" — 175
"Snowy Mountains Slopes" — 171
Society for the Preservation of Windmills — 149
Society of Canadian Artists — 72
"Souris River" — 25
South Kensington Art School (London) — 71, 83
Southern Alberta Institute of Technology and Art (Calgary) — 104, 149, 193, 194
Southesk, Earl of — 11
"Spring Reflections" — 175
"Spring Thaw" — 211
"Stacked Road" — 212
Stegner, Wallace — 14
Stevenson, W. L. — 193-95, 215
Stone, Andrew J. — 171
"Straw Stacks, March Thaw" — 197
"Summer Trees" — 194
"Sunny Alberta" — 215
"Sunset, Metlaskatla" — 26
"Sutherland Trail" — 143
Symons, Gardner — 152

"Tangle of Fallen Trees" — 171
Technique of the Colour Woodcut, The — 104
"The Arbutus Trees, Saanich, B.C." — 198
"The Encampment, Rocky Mountains" — 25
"The Great Cañon" — 30
"The Inland Passage, B.C." — 79
"The Jackpine" — 127
"The Marsh, Emma Lake" — 143
"The Mighty Fraser" — 101
"The Old Cypress" — 193
"The Road in the Valley" — 143
"The Three Sisters" — 74
"The Valley in Winter" — 143
"The Winding River Fraser" — 101
Tobey, Mark — 101, 184
Toronto Art School — 71
Toronto *Mail and Empire* — 97
"Train in the Mountains" — 68
Transcontinental Survey — 73
Treaty No. 7 — 38
"Trees and Lake" — 143
"Trial Island from near Victoria" — 68
Trinity Medical College (Toronto) — 37

Twenties Group — 194

Uhthoff, Ina D. D. — 98, 101, 104
United States-Canadian Boundary Survey — 18, 26
United States Geodesic Survey in the Northwest — 79
United States Hydrographic Survey — 26
University of Alberta — 200, 212
University of British Columbia — 209
University of Calgary — 197
University of Iowa — 212
University of Manitoba — 212
University of Saskatchewan — 127, 140, 209, 211, 212
University of Toronto — 37, 48
University of Wisconsin — 211
Upper Canada College (Toronto) — 56
Urushibara, Y. — 104

"Valley of the South Fork, Old Man's River" — 38
"Valley Road, Winter" — 197
Van Horne, William — 48, 56
Vancouver Art Gallery — 193, 194
Vancouver School of Art — 98, 197, 209
"Vapours Round the Mountain Curled" — 119
Varley, F. H. — 98, 195
Victoria School of Art — 101
Victoria University (Cobourg, Ontario) — 48
"View of Edmonton from the North Saskatchewan River" — 150

Wanderings of an Artist — 18
Warre, Captain Henry — 18
Week, The — 183
Western Union Telegraph Expedition — 18, 28, 30
Westminster School of Art (London) — 183, 197
West Shore — 79
Whistler, James A. — 73
Whymper, Frederick — 30
Williams, W. H. — 11
"Windswept" — 143
Winnipeg Art School — 209
Winnipeg *Tribune* — 104
Winnipeg *Free Press* — 72
"Winter Moonlight" — 193
"Winter Scene" — 94

Edited by D. Scollard
Photographs by Ron Marsh
Designed by Bill Little
Typesetting by Offset Services Limited
Colour Separations for Lithography by Herzig Somerville Limited
Printed by Sampson Matthews Limited
Bound by The Hunter Rose Company